AN AMERICAN DREAM

Books by John W. Whitehead

The Separation Illusion

Schools on Fire (with Jon T. Barton)

The New Tyranny

The Second American Revolution

*The Freedom of Religious Expression
in Public Universities
and High Schools*

The Stealing of America

*Home Education and Constitutional Liberties:
The Historical and Constitutional Arguments in Support of
Home Instruction*
(with Wendell R. Bird)

The Right to Picket and the Freedom of Public Discourse

Parents' Rights

The End of Man

An American Dream

AN AMERICAN DREAM

John W. Whitehead

CROSSWAY BOOKS • WESTCHESTER, ILLINOIS
A DIVISION OF GOOD NEWS PUBLISHERS

First printing, 1987

Printed in the United States of America

Library of Congress Catalog Card Number 86-72067

ISBN 0-89107-422-8

To Charles A. McIlhenny, D.Min.

CONTENTS

ACKNOWLEDGMENTS

*A*s with a play, so it is with a book: there are many supporting players who assist the main performer. This is true of the present book.

I would first like to express my gratitude to my faithful wife, Carol, and my five children: Jayson, Jonathan, Elisabeth, Joel, and Joshua. They always carry the ultimate burden of living with me while writing my books. Without their patience, prayers, and assistance, there would be no books.

I appreciate very much the support of Crossway Books— especially Lane and Jan Dennis.

F. Tayton Dencer's comments and suggestions were very helpful. Thanks to Daniel Dreisbach for his research and astute suggestions. Rebecca Beane's suggestions and proofreading of the galleys were valuable. Also, my gratitude goes to John Messina and Kimberly Roberts for research assistance and to Ken Clark for his work on the footnotes and bibliography. Sandra Sample's typing is appreciated.

Finally, I owe a great debt to the many scholars I relied on in my research. These include Alice Baldwin, Clinton Rossiter, Herbert Foster, and others. Ecclesiastes tells us that there is nothing new under the sun. This is, I believe, an absolute truth and applies aptly to my work as well as to all those dead and living.

AUTHOR'S FOREWORD

I have heard the phrase "American dream" bantered about since I was a small child. Curiously enough, the phrase is very seldom defined, and when it is, it is usually couched in materialistic terms such as the "dream" of owning a new house or a new car. This type of banal thinking is very appropriate for the present age, but it is distinctly foreign to the way men and women first dreamed about what America should be.

It seems rather odd that in a little over two hundred years the original ideas that undergirded the freedoms and liberties we enjoy should be so quickly lost. Part of this is because things do change and a nation's people do alter what they believe is important. However, it is also due in part to the prejudice and often lack of intellectual integrity modern historians bring to the subject of our country's origins. This means that children in the public schools are not given an accurate picture of American historical beginnings. As a result, the great majority of modern Americans have lost any concept of what it means to be an American as well as what America itself should mean to the world and the future of freedom.

Realistically speaking, we do live in perilous times. In saying this, I am not attempting to be pessimistic or to portray a doomsday vision for America. However, in such a time as this we must be honest and, in turn, seek to find ways to assure the future freedoms of the peoples of the world.

Since, as mere humans, we cannot divine principles from the future, we are forced to look to the past to see if there is anything there that can aid us. In this endeavor there are no golden ages. We cannot relive the past. Moreover, if we were somehow transported back to 1776, for example, we would quickly find that the American colonists were not gods but people with real problems struggling to get by much as we are today.

Nevertheless, there were times when certain principles were enunciated which do offer hopes and freedom. The founding of America was one such time. It should be remembered, however, that even if these principles were restored in modern American culture, things may have changed to such a degree that their application may not bring about the same results as they did in the eighteenth and nineteenth centuries.

In writing this book I realize I have opened myself to criticism of certain facts and how I have presented them. Moreover, I have not attempted to force a particular historical, theological, or political view onto the reader. That is not the reason for this book. I have simply tried to stick to the facts and let them speak for themselves.

In this presentation I focus on a certain religious aspect of colonial culture, rather than economics or other subjects, because religion was one of the more profound phenomena affecting colonial Americans. This is not to say that other forces were not important; but they are not the focus of this book. I do, however, end the book with my views of how we may strengthen the things that do remain. At that juncture, I may be criticized for clearly stating my point of view.

Although I write this book for the present age, my heart lies with the children who will be compelled either to live out the mistakes of our day or build upon solid principles that we can formulate. And if we cannot or refuse to formulate these principles and live them out in practice, we may see that our children are chained not only to our inadvertence but also to our willful disregard of the truth.

John W. Whitehead
Manassas, Virginia
January 1987

PART ONE

AMERICAN TUNE

We come on a ship they call the
  Mayflower
We come on the ship that sailed the
  moon
We come in the age's most uncer-
  tain hour
And sing an American tune
But it's all right, it's all right
You can't be forever blessed.

Paul Simon
"American Tune" (1973)

THE "ACCIDENT"

*A*merica may turn out to be an historical accident—a brief parenthesis that is closing before our eyes. This can be seen in the numerous end-time scenarios that pervade the culture.

Paul Simon aptly summed up this mood in his song "American Tune":

> I don't know a soul who's not been battered
> I don't have a friend who feels at ease
> I don't know a dream that's not been shattered
> or driven to its knees
> But it's all right, it's all right
> We've lived so well so long
> Still, when I think of the road
> we're traveling on
> I wonder what went wrong
> I can't help it, I wonder what went wrong.[1]

These lyrics, written at the height of the Watergate scandal of the early 1970s, more accurately portray the mood of modern America now than when they were written. The "Age of Aquarius" did not follow on the heels of the sixties. Instead of the dawning of a new age, frustration followed. Next came the apathy and smug materialism of the eighties. The hope for a new beginning has waned.

Likewise, the freedom that America supposedly stands for seems to be fading on a worldwide scale. A large portion of the world's population is, at present, living under oppression. Leaders in Iron Curtain, Third World, Eastern Asia, and Southern

Hemisphere countries manipulate, control, and often terrorize their countrymen.

The so-called free societies of the West are also on the decline. In fact, Jean-François Revel in *How Democracies Perish* pessimistically notes that the entire concept of democracy may soon be obliterated. Revel elaborates concerning the decline of democracy:

> In its modern sense of a form of society reconciling governmental efficiency with legitimacy, authority with individual freedoms, it will have lasted a little over two centuries, to judge by the speed of growth of the forces bent on its destruction. And, really, only a tiny minority of the human race will have experienced it. In both time and space, democracy fills a very small corner. The span of roughly two hundred years applies only to the few countries where it first appeared, still very incomplete, at the end of the eighteenth century. Most of the other countries in which democracy exists adopted it under a century ago, under a half a century ago, in some cases less than a decade ago.[2]

Why does Revel feel that democracy is headed toward destruction? He notes:

> Democracy probably could have endured had it been the only type of political organization in the world. But it is not basically structured to defend itself against outside enemies seeking its annihilation, especially since the latest and most dangerous of these external enemies, communism—the current and complete model of totalitarianism—parades as democracy perfected when it is in fact the absolute negation of democracy.
>
> Democracy is by its very nature turned inward. Its vocation is the patient and realistic improvement of life in a community. Communism, on the other hand, necessarily looks outward because it is a failed society and is incapable of engendering a viable one. The Nomenklatura, the body of bureaucrat-dictators who govern the system, has no choice, therefore, but to direct its abilities toward expansion abroad. Communism is more skillful, more persevering than democracy in defending itself. Democracy tends to ignore, even

deny, threats to its existence because it loathes doing what is needed to counter them. It awakens only when the danger becomes deadly, imminent, evident. By then, either there is too little time left for it to save itself, or the price of survival has become crushingly high.[3]

Mankind's greatest quest—liberty and freedom—seems in most instances to be an unreachable dream. And even where liberty, freedom, and equality form the battle cry of a revolutionary people, the result is often unspeakable horrors. We see this very clearly in the French Revolution (1789), as well as in numerous "liberation" movements of our day.

Of course, the most obvious question concerning the elusive nature of freedom is why it seems almost inevitable that people are doomed to a form of slavery instead of experiencing liberty. Why do people tyrannized in such states as the Soviet Union seem to languish on in oppression with little resistance? As early as 1776, Thomas Jefferson in the Declaration of Independence wrote that "all experience hath shown that mankind are more disposed to suffer, while evils are sufferable, than to right themselves by abolishing the forms to which they are accustomed."

Aleksandr Solzhenitsyn speaks eloquently on this subject. He tells of the Russian people kneeling inside the doors of their apartments, pressing their ears to listen when the KGB (Soviet secret police) came at midnight to arrest a neighbor. He comments that if all the people had come out and driven off the officers, sheer public opinion would have demoralized the effort to subdue what should be a free people. But the people hid and trembled.

THE SOUL

In America the ideals of freedom and liberty have been realized more fully than in any other time in history. America, however, appears to be a shrinking island of freedom. A looming authoritarianism threatens the United States, and Americans are beginning to feel the squeeze of the iron hand, albeit clothed in a velvet glove. Faced with this situation, we are tempted to ask why we are losing our freedoms. But the more central question is, how did America ever establish a free country wherein a people could boast of not only the right to freedom but also the right to openly challenge the actions of the state? The answer has its roots in the traditional religion of the American people.

Harvard professor Harvey Cox in *The Seduction of the Spirit* writes: "Ultimately a people's religion, no matter how it has been composed, becomes that people's own 'soul.' Whatever inner contradictions it houses, it serves an essential purpose for those whose collective consciousness it represented. When the 'soul' departs, as mortals have known since the beginning of time, the body soon dies too."[4] The soul of the American people has been the Christian religion in its various forms. It provided the people with a common morality which allowed individual freedom within moral constraints—a common morality altogether absent in the present American society.

From those who crossed the Atlantic on the *Mayflower* up to the modern television evangelists, Christianity has been the main religious stream flowing through the American consciousness. It has served as a *de facto* establishment of religion in America. This is true no matter how many attempts have been made to disestablish the Christian religion. Even in contemporary secular America, shadowy vestiges of Christianity remain. These are expressed largely through civil religion and its attendant public affirmations of the belief in God and the Bible.

Modern Christianity, because of its shallowness and devalued spirituality, differs significantly from the earlier Christian experiences of the seventeenth and eighteenth centuries. Its lack of spiritual depth renders modern Christianity nearly powerless to shape and influence contemporary American culture. Yet Christianity was not always so ineffectual. Early American Christianity profoundly affected social institutions. This is the natural consequence of a dynamic spirituality. However, Christianity no longer has much impact on the major social institutions. The very soul of America, as Cox notes, seems to be atrophying. Thus, the body may soon die also.

AN AMERICAN DREAM

America began with a dream, a dream greatly shaped and informed by Christianity. This dream, the American dream, is what has made the rest of the world look to America in hope. Yet, though we often hear about the American dream, it is seldom defined. What exactly is it?

The American dream consists of three basic fundamental concepts. They are rights, resistance, and a future optimism as they are undergirded by the traditional religion. This future optimism was once called millennialism or what some today may refer to as utopianism. These three themes run throughout the history of this country. Their current demise is peculiar to modern-day America.

G. K. Chesterton in 1922 remarked that America is "a nation with the soul of a church . . . the only nation in the world that is founded on a creed. That creed is set forth with dogmatic and even theological lucidity in the Declaration of Independence."[5] The American dream, then, is best expressed in America's only true creedal document—the Declaration of Independence. In the Declaration of Independence we find the three themes of rights, resistance, and future optimism which have been repeated over the past two hundred years. They have been restated on numerous occasions by the American people as well as American leadership, especially presidents and other government officials in public addresses.

However, the Declaration does not stand alone. Over a century of teaching and preaching by the colonial clergy and others preceded the words that fill the pages of the document. Without an accurate understanding of those who proclaimed and fought for freedom in the years preceding 1776, the Declaration of Independence makes little sense.

Thus, the Declaration of Independence, and the history which preceded it, is where one must seek the content of what we have come to call the American dream. If there is to be any semblance of political freedom and optimism for the future, it is this author's opinion that we must recapture the ideals that are set forth in this document. Yet, even if these ideals are recaptured, contemporary society may be too rancid to restore freedom. Nevertheless, our task must be to attempt such a recovery, at least for freedom's sake.

If not, the American tune may soon be only a faint whisper in a storm of totalitarianism. Worse yet, it may be an accident in freedom and a dream that has relapsed to a nightmare.

THE AMERICAN MIND

O n May 26, 1776, that indefatigable correspondent John Adams (1735-1826), who represented Massachusetts at the Second Continental Congress, wrote exultantly to his friend James Warren that "every post and every day rolls in upon us independence like a torrent."[1] Adams had reason for rejoicing, for this was what he and others had hoped and worked for almost since the Congress had convened in May of the previous year. It helped, to be sure, that George III (1738-1820) had proclaimed the colonies in rebellion and thus encouraged the Americans to take him at his word. Later, George Washington (1732-1799) proceeded to drive General Howe out of Boston. This demonstrated that Americans need not stand on the defensive, but could vindicate themselves in military strategy quite as well as in political.

However exciting to some, America was going through the difficult process of being born. In any event, the stage of history was being set. On June 7, 1776, Richard Henry Lee (1732-1794) of Virginia introduced three resolutions calling for independence, foreign alliances, and confederation. Some wanted unity and voted to postpone the final vote for three weeks. This allowed time for debate and for the hesitant and fainthearted to come over or step out. Meantime, Congress appointed a committee to prepare "a Declaration of Independence." This committee consisted of Benjamin Franklin (1706-1790), John Adams, Roger Sherman (1721-1793), Robert Livingston (1746-1813), and Thomas Jefferson (1743-1826).

Jefferson had come to the Continental Congress the previous

year bringing with him a reputation for literature, science, and a talent for composition. His writings, said John Adams, "were remarkable for their peculiar felicity of expression."[2] In part because of his rhetorical gifts, in part because he already had a reputation of working quickly, in part because it was thought that Virginia, as the oldest, the largest, and the most deeply committed of the states, should take the lead, the committee unanimously turned to Jefferson to prepare a draft declaration.

We know a great deal about the composition of that draft. Jefferson wrote it standing at his desk (still preserved) in the second-floor parlor of a young German bricklayer named Graff, and he completed it in two weeks. We have his word for it that he "turned neither to book nor pamphlet" and that all the authority of the Declaration "rests on the harmonizing sentiments of the day, whether expressed in conversation, in letters, printed essays, or in the elementary books of public right, as Aristotle, Cicero, Locke, Sidney, etc."[3] We can accept Jefferson's statement made fifty years later that the object of the Declaration was to be "an appeal to the tribunal of the world"—that "decent respect to the opinions of Mankind" invoked in the Declaration itself. However, in Jefferson's words (as he wrote to James Madison in 1823), it certainly was "not to find out new principles, or new arguments, never before thought of; not merely to say things which had never been said before; but to place before mankind the common sense of the subject, in terms so plain and firm as to command their assent, and to justify ourselves in the independent stand we are compelled to take. Neither aiming at originality of principle or sentiment, nor yet copied from any particular and previous writing, it was intended to be an *expression of the American mind*, and to give to that expression the proper tone and spirit called for by the occasion."[4]

The Declaration of Independence, then, was an expression of the American mind that was prevalent in the colonies of that time. As Jefferson stated, the Declaration contained no new ideas, nor was there any originality in it on his part. He merely articulated what people of that day were thinking.

A WAY OF THINKING

The American mind, or the basic elements in the American dream, are set forth in the two opening paragraphs of the Declaration of Independence. The Declaration opens by stating:

When in the Course of human events, it becomes necessary for one people to dissolve the political bands, which have connected them with another, and to assume among the powers of the earth, the separate and equal station to which the Laws of Nature and of Nature's God entitle them, a decent respect to the opinions of mankind requires that they should declare the causes which impel them to the separation.

The opening paragraph of the Declaration states that the colonists are impelled or required to separate from Great Britain for certain reasons:

We hold these truths to be self-evident, that all men are created equal, that they are endowed by their Creator with certain unalienable Rights, that among these are Life, Liberty and the pursuit of Happiness.—That to secure these rights, Governments are instituted among Men, deriving their just powers from the consent of the governed,—That whenever any Form of Government becomes destructive of these ends, it is the Right of the People to alter or to abolish it, and to institute new Government, laying its foundation on such principles and organizing its powers in such form, as to them shall seem most likely to effect their Safety and Happiness. Prudence, indeed, will dictate that Governments long established should not be changed for light and transient causes; and accordingly all experience hath shewn, that mankind are more disposed to suffer, while evils are sufferable, than to right themselves by abolishing the forms to which they are accustomed. But when a long train of abuses and usurpations, pursuing invariably the same Object evinces a design to reduce them under absolute Despotism, it is their right, it is their duty, to throw off such Government, and to provide new Guards for their future security.—Such has been the patient sufferance of these Colonies; and such is now the necessity which constrains them to alter their former Systems of Government. The history of the present King of Great Britain is a history of repeated injuries and usurpations, all having in direct object the establishment of an absolute Tyranny over these States. To prove this, let Facts be submitted to a candid world.[5]

This preamble sums up with lucidity, logic, and eloquence the philosophy which presided over the argument for the American Revolution, the creation of a new political system, and the vindication of the rights of man—all in less than two hundred words. Here we find expressed what is universal rather than parochial, what is permanent rather than transient, in the American Revolution. Where most of the body of the Declaration is retrospective, the preamble is prospective. In the years to come, it would be translated into the basic institutions of the American republic, and would form the basis of the American dream.

Consider the opening words of the Declaration: "When, in the Course of human events . . ." That places it, and the Revolution, at once in the appropriate setting, against the background of not merely American or British but universal history. That connects it with the experience of people everywhere—not only at a moment of history, but in every era. This concept of the place of American history is underlined by successive phrases of the opening sentence. It points to a future of hope and optimism.

Thus, the new nation is to assume its place "among the powers of the earth." It is not the laws of the British empire, or even of history, but of "Nature and of Nature's God" which entitled Americans to an equal station. Moreover, it is "a decent respect to the opinions of mankind" that requires this justification. No other political document of the eighteenth century proclaims so broad a purpose. No political document of our own day associates the United States so boldly with universal history in the cosmic system.

FORGETTING THE PAST

Few will dispute the fact that Americans generally have lost the awareness that their republic began with a "revolution." Not long ago a group of students in Indianapolis showed copies of the Declaration of Independence to several hundred people and asked them to sign it. Most refused, stating that it sounded rather "dangerous."[6] In July 1975, the People's Bicentennial Commission handed out copies of the Declaration of Independence in downtown Denver without identifying it. Only one in five persons even recognized it, and one man said: "There is so much of this revolutionary stuff going on now. I can't stand it."[7]

The dreams of an earlier generation of Americans were obviously quite different. Alexis de Tocqueville (1805-1859) wrote of these early Americans with admiration in 1835: "In that land the great experiment of the attempt to construct society upon a new basis was made by civilized man; and it was there, for the first time, that theories hitherto unknown, or deemed impracticable, were to exhibit a spectacle for which the world had not been prepared by the history of the past."[8]

"REVOLUTION"

When the colonists spoke of "revolution," it was not used in the sense it is used today. Revolution to them was not the over-throwing of established government, but *resistance* to the illegitimate acts of a government predisposed to tyranny.

Moreover, the colonists did not rebel in the true sense of the word. Modern historians seldom mention that Great Britain broke off relations with the colonies and declared war against them. This was officially done through the Prohibitory Act passed by the British Parliament on November 20, 1775. This Act prohibited all trade with America, impressed American sailors into the British Navy, and made all American ships subject to confiscation as if they were the ships and effects of "open enemies." In addition, countries and other British colonies attempting to trade with the thirteen American colonies would be treated as "open enemies." The Act was a declaration of unrestricted warfare against a "foreign" enemy—the American colonies.

Concerning the Prohibitory Act, John Adams wrote to an acquaintance:

> I know not whether you have seen the Act of Parliament called the restraining Act, or prohibitory Act, or piratical Act, or plundering Act, or Act of Independency, for by all of these titles is it called. I think the most apposite is the Act of Independency, for King, Lords and Commons have united in sundering this country from that I think forever. It is a compleat Dismemberment of the British Empire. It throws thirteen colonies out of the Royal Protection, levels all distinctions, and makes us independent in spight of our supplications and entreaties.[9]

As seen by Adams, not only the British Parliament but also some colonial leaders recognized that this act severed the colonies from the king. For the first time, the colonists began to hold the king personally responsible for threatening their liberties. This fact, with other oppressive actions of the British Empire, forced the colonists to respond with *defensive* resistance.

In actuality, the American Revolution was "a revolution to preserve a social order rather than to change it."[10] As Daniel Boorstin writes:

> The most obvious peculiarity of our American Revolution is that, in the modern European sense of the word, it was hardly a revolution at all. The Daughters of the American Revolution, who have been understandably sensitive on this subject, have always insisted in their literature that the American Revolution was no revolution but merely a colonial rebellion. The more I have looked into the subject, the more convinced I have become of the wisdom of their naivete.[11]

Moreover, as Peter Drucker notes, the American resistance was a "conservative counterrevolution."[12] As such, Drucker writes: "The American Revolution brought victory and power to a group which in Europe had been almost completely defeated and which was apparently dying out rapidly: the anticentralist, antitotalitarian conservatives with their hostility to absolute and centralized government and their distrust of any ruler claiming perfection."[13] The success of the American Revolution, adds Drucker, defeated the Enlightenment in England and enabled conservative thought to gain ascendancy there.[14]

In light of this, Drucker challenged the belief that the origins of the American Revolution were to be found in pure Enlightenment thinking in denying that the American Revolution was a forerunner of the French. He asserted:

> In intention and effect it was a successful countermovement against the very rationalist despotism of the Enlightenment which provided the political foundation for the French Revolution. Though the French Revolution happened later in time, it had politically and philosophically been anticipated by the American Revolution. The conservatives of 1776 and 1787 fought and overcame the spirit of the French Revolution so that the American development actually represents a more advanced stage in history than the *Etats Generaux*, the

Terror, and Napoleon. Far from being a revolt against the old tyranny of feudalism, the American Revolution was a conservative counterrevolution in the name of freedom against the new tyranny of rationalist liberalism and Enlightened Despotism.[15]

There were five essential differences between the two "revolutions." First, the American Revolution was grounded firmly upon established legal principles and traditions, whereas the French Revolution moved on obviously illegal and unprincipled premises. Second, the American Revolution was *defensive*, a battle by Americans to preserve their liberties and continue their legitimate development, whereas the French was from the beginning an offensive revolution. Third, the American Revolution had a fixed, definite, limited, and particularistic objective, whereas the French had none and moved in terms of arbitrary will and boundless anarchy. Fourth, the American Revolution, because of its limited and legal nature, met with limited resistance, whereas the French could only force its way by violence and crimes.[16] Fifth, the French Revolution was anticlerical and antichurch, while the American Revolution was not only supported by the clergy but was incited by the colonial ministers.

SELF-EVIDENT TRUTHS
Let us now turn to those principles that Jefferson called "self-evident truths." That phrase, too, is an expression of the American mind. Unfortunately, modern Americans, steeped in relativism, would not assume that there is a body of "self-evident truths"—certainly not in the area of government or politics. Truths today must earn their way, as it were, having to submit their credentials to the test of the laboratory and the computer. Moreover, even if they pass these, they are regarded with suspicion and confined to strict limits of time and place. The colonists, however, because of the influence of Christianity, were confident that the reason of man could penetrate to ultimate truth, and that that truth, once discovered (or apprehended), was not only as self-evident as a maxim of Euclid, but was both permanent and universal. As historian Clinton Rossiter has recognized:

> The colonial mind was thoroughly Christian in its approach to education, philosophy, and social theory. . . . The Chris-

tian religion grew less influential as the colonies moved toward maturity and liberty. Yet this decline in influence was only relative; the variants of Christianity remained a primary determinant of the culture of every class and section.[17]

The American mind of the colonial period did not acknowledge a different order of truth, one for the lofty realms of mathematics, another for the more earthbound regions, and still another for society, politics, and the economy. While clearly discernible in the natural world, the cause of "Nature and of Nature's God" applied equally to the world of politics and to the law. Benjamin Franklin, as a young man, said:

How exact and regular is everything in the *natural* World! How wisely in every part contriv'd. We cannot here find the least Defect. Those who have studied the mere animal and vegetable Creation demonstrate that nothing can be more harmonious and beautiful! All the heavenly bodies, the Stars and Planets, are regulated with the utmost Wisdom! And can we suppose less care to be taken in the Order of the Moral than in the natural System?[18]

Therefore, self-evident truths could exist in a society that still adhered to absolutes. In modern relativistic society, however, there can be no such thing. To Jefferson, these self-evident truths formed a total reality. He listed seven of them:

1. That all men are created equal;
2. That men are endowed by the Creator with "unalienable" rights;
3. That these rights include life, liberty, and the pursuit of happiness;
4. That it is to secure these rights that government is instituted among men;
5. That governments are instituted to derive their powers from the consent of the governed;
6. That when a form of government becomes destructive of these ends, it becomes illegitimate and men may alter or abolish it; and,
7. That men have the right, then, to institute new governments designed to effect their safety and happiness.

It is clear that the rights and hopes set forth in these self-evident truths are based on a religious view of life. That is not to say that Americans did not draw from other than Christian sources in formulating these fundamental principles. To the contrary, the colonists drew from many different sources to effectuate the principles that are enunciated in the Declaration and that have become embodied in the modern concept of the American dream. As Henry Steele Commager writes:

> What Americans did was more important than invent new principles; in the telling phrase of John Adams, "they *realized* the theories of the wisest writers." They actualized them, they legalized them, they institutionalized them. That was, and remains, the supreme achievement of the American Revolution; indeed, in the longer perspective, that *was* and *is* the American Revolution.[19]

Men speak not only in verbal language but also in the language of history—in the context and meaning of their time and place. It was the language of American colonial history which was written into the Declaration of Independence and other documents that were to follow. These drew upon not only the European and classical sources so often cited by the shapers of American history, John Locke (1632-1704) and Baron de Montesquieu (1689-1755), but also Aristotle, Cicero, Plutarch, Hobbes, Burlamaqui, John Milton (1608-1674), Hooker, David Hume (1711-1776), Bolingbroke, William Blackstone (1723-1780), Burke, Shaftesbury, and a score of collateral branches. As James Burnham notes:

> But the Fathers were the masters, not the victims, of these inherited ideas, and sometimes it is the rhetoric more than the ideas that is taken over. The Fathers were protected from ideology not only by piety and a native skepticism toward abstract reason, but by their persistent sense of fact, of the specific.[20]

The language of "Reason" and "Nature" had a long philosophical and legal history and was by no means the exclusive property of the Enlightenment writers. For example, in 1644 the

Presbyterian Samuel Rutherford, in *Lex Rex,* cited Aristotle and Aquinas and appealed to "God and Nature."[21] Many of the early European Christian writers, and later the American clergy, asserted that the law of nature supersedes all institutions but was elucidated in the Bible.

Moreover, many men use words which to others imply a religious view not held by the speaker or writer without an awareness either of the divergence of meaning or the mixed presuppositions. Witness, for example, Reverend John Witherspoon (1722-1794), an influential Presbyterian leader who in 1768 assumed the presidency of the College of New Jersey (now Princeton University). An orthodox Calvinist, Witherspoon, without any sense of contradiction, spoke in the language of rights and reason, combining it with his Christianity.[22]

In spite of this pragmatic usage, there was, however, an element of philosophical indistinction which must be recognized. The epistemological awareness developed over the last two centuries cannot be read back into the colonial period; nor, on the other hand, can modern secularism be so read into the philosophy of the Declaration of Independence. To speak therefore of an "American Enlightenment" is to attempt to read into the Revolution later developments in American thought.

PROBLEMS

Ideas beget a progeny which soon outstrips the narrow concepts of their creator. This is, in a special degree, true of the philosophy of the American colonists.

A concept of both the Declaration of Independence and the American dream is that all men are created equal. This phrase was developed and written in a time when the American colonies labored under the enigma and curse of the slavery of Black citizens.

America in 1776 as well as in 1787 (the time of the drafting of the Constitution) was a slave state in apparent contradiction of what many of the framers proclaimed. The same Thomas Jefferson who, for instance, could rhetorically claim that "all men are created equal" in the Declaration of Independence possessed, at that time, Black slaves. "How is it," Dr. Samuel Johnson (1709-1784) mused, "that we hear the loudest yelps for liberty from the drivers of Negroes?"[23]

In fairness to Jefferson, it must be noted that he did provide an antislavery section in an initial draft of the Declaration of Independence. Unfortunately, this section was later removed by Congress, against the protests of Jefferson.[24]

Of course, there will always be contradictions wherever men and women exist. This was true of the American colonists. They were not perfect men and women. This is the plight of fallen people. However, that does not invalidate the concepts enunciated in the Declaration of Independence. Stated in the Declaration of Independence, and as they became part of the American culture, the concepts and ideas take on a universal meaning. In essence, the ideas have escaped from the pages of the document and have entered the flow of cosmic history.

This is not to say that the evil of slavery should be excused; nor is it to say that any injustices perpetrated by any society are to be glossed over. What we must recognize is that the self-evident truths articulated have a meaning that extends far beyond the human circumstances in which they were enunciated.

Too often modern historians, many of them Christian, denigrate America's beginnings because of such problems. Such meanderings elude reality. What must be recognized is that without the religious undergirding that allowed for the promulgation of these self-evident truths, Americans could today be living in a much different society where the very concept of self-evident truths would be only a shadow in the corridors of authoritarianism.

OLD-TIME RELIGION

All who have studied American history agree that there would be no self-evident truths and they would not have been so clearly set forth and have become an integral part of the American culture without the Christian religion. The predominance of the Christian religion in colonial America cannot be denied. The dispute over Christianity's role in shaping American society has to do with how much direct influence and impact it actually had.

There are two distinct approaches that have been employed by those who attempt to diminish the influence of the Christian religion on American origins. The first approach does not even mention the influence of religion on the early formation of the ideas of the American people. The second approach readily acknowledges that the Christian religion had influence, but says it was negligible. Both these approaches are doubtful.

On the other hand, to acknowledge that the Christian religion did heavily influence colonial writings, even the Declaration of Independence, in the formation of the American dream does not mean one views American origins in terms of a theocracy or what some have come to call the theory of "Christian America." The only attempt at establishing a theocracy in America occurred in Puritan Massachusetts. It failed.

There can be, in all likelihood, no such thing as a "Christian nation" in our time. Moreover, there are, in the author's opinion, problems with the idea that a nation could be Christian in the sense of what the Bible terms "Christian." Again, this does not mean that Christianity or any religion cannot have a tremendous influence on developing the ideas and thought forms of a culture.

To the contrary, the history of the late 1600s and early 1700s indicates that there was one particular group of leaders that did have a tremendous influence on the formation of the American dream and the ideas that flowed into the Declaration of Independence. This was the clergy. It was their "old-time religion" that led to many of the rights, freedoms, and beliefs that we hold sacred today in modern society. Their preaching and writing became, in essence, the American mind.

PART TWO

THE DREAM

When our liberty is invaded and struck at, 'tis sufficient reason for our making war for the defence or recovery of it. Liberty is one of the most sacred and inviolable privileges mankind enjoy; without it life itself is insipid and many times burdensome. For what comfort can a man take in life when at the disposal of a despotic and arbitrary tyrant, who has no other law but his will? . . . I would entreat you to see to it that you engage in so noble a cause for right ends. Let your principal motives be the honor of God, and the defence of your country. Fight for liberty against slavery.

Reverend James Cogswell (1757)

THE CLERGY

*T*he New England clergy of the eighteenth century occupied a position of peculiar influence and power in the life of their own communities and of the American colonies.[1] As Alice M. Baldwin recognized: "It is true that they had lost something of the respect and reverence as well as much of the political power which they had enjoyed in the first sixty years of settlement and expansion. Nevertheless, it is unsafe to conclude that their parishioners did not on the whole respect them and that their influence was small. There is abundant evidence to the contrary."[2]

If we are to have an objective view of prerevolutionary philosophy, we must realize that the "dissenting" clergy, especially the Calvinistically inclined clergy of New England, were among the chief agitators of the American Revolution (and, after it began, among the most zealous and successful in keeping it alive). These clergy played an important part in teaching *political theory* to the people and in giving to the theories religious sanction. And this occurred well before 1776.

Calvinistic *political* philosophy (not so much Calvinistic theology) was a driving force in prerevolutionary colonial thinking for several reasons. First, as one historian writes: "Approximately three-fourths of the colonists at the time of the Revolution were identified with denominations that had arisen from the Reformed, Puritan wing of European Protestantism: Congregationalism, Presbyterianism, Baptists, German and Dutch Reformed."[3] Further, it should be remembered that "throughout the colonial period the great majority of the people in all the New England colonies except Rhode Island were Congregationalists, who sometimes and in some places approached so closely to Presbyterianism that it is hard to distinguish accurately between the two [denominations]."⁴ These denominations were primarily Calvinistic in their orientation.

Second, this fact is important because these dominant denominations, because of their Calvinistic background, were open to the European philosophy, largely Calvinistic in origin, that played an important part in structuring the thought forms that would undergird the American Revolution. As such, the Calvinistic clergy was partly responsible for passing on the ingredients of the American dream—rights, resistance and future optimism—to the people of the colonies.

There is no attempt here to say that Calvinism was the only force operating in the minds of the clergy; nor is it to argue that Calvinism, or any of its political derivatives, is a correct theological view or that it represents true Christian thinking. It is presented merely as one influential driving force in developing the American mind and dream.

A "LEARNED CLERGY"

The New England clergy were the most influential leaders of their day, influencing the minds of many of those who formulated the ideas that led to the break with Great Britain. They were for the most part a "learned clergy," graduates of Harvard or of Yale.⁵ For example, of the fifty-two settled Congregational ministers of New Hampshire in 1764, forty-eight were college graduates.⁶ Moreover, from 1748 to 1800, nine-tenths were college graduates.⁷

Shortly after graduation, the young ministers were settled in their new parishes, where they often remained throughout their lives. Sometimes they were given land, money, or some other special inducement to settle and were usually promised a salary which, when paid regularly, meant comfort at least. But frequently the salary was inadequate or paid in depreciating currency and at best was none too large to meet the demands of such position. For the most part the ministers lived in small towns or smaller villages and stretched their salaries to the family needs by farming or by taking into their homes a few boys whom they fitted for college or training for the ministry. Here they lived among their people, on weekdays settling disputes and occasionally, in the remoter districts, serving as doctor or even as village lawyer or schoolteacher, on the Sabbath preaching to men and women whose lives they intimately shared. As Baldwin concludes:

> They were sober and industrious in their ways, usually dignified in their bearing, and they spoke as men having authority. "You must expect if you come to Danbury to be a good deal noticed and perhaps gazed at," wrote young Ebenezer Baldwin in 1763 to his sister Bethiah, "for to be the Minister's sister you know in a Country Town is a considerable thing."[8]

SERMONS: TEACHING THE PEOPLE

In colonial America there were few newspapers and fewer books. How different it must have been from our media-dominated age. The sermon delivered by the local minister was the basic, and many times only, form of communication for the colonists. "[T]he New England Sermon," writes historian Harry S. Stout, had a "topical range and social influence . . . so powerful in shaping cultural values, meanings, and a sense of corporate purpose that even television pales in comparison":

> Unlike modern mass media, the sermon stood alone in local New England contexts as the regular (at least weekly) medium of public communication. As a channel of information, it combined religious, educational, and journalistic functions, and supplied all the key terms necessary to understand existence in this world and the next. As the only event in public assembly that regularly brought the entire community together, it also represented the central ritual of social order and control.[9]

The ministers who attended the annual ministerial conventions or at least the meetings of the local associations, who read more than most of their neighbors, who corresponded with their fellow ministers and men of other towns and colonies, who had often been the classmates and remained the friends of the rising young lawyers and merchants, were likely to be the primary means of contact between their parishioners and the outside world. As teachers who prepared the more ambitious young men for college, they had the opportunity to impress them with their own beliefs.

As preachers they had at least a weekly opportunity to reach most of the people living in the parish, who, if not church members, were usually church attendants. They preached not only on Sunday but on many special occasions prescribed by the churches or ordered by the colonial assemblies, such as days of fasting and prayer and days of thanksgiving:

> If special news arrived, such as the death of the King, a defeat or a victory in war, the minister was likely to make the most of it, and to his country audience a sermon on such a theme must have been especially welcome. Here was a fine opportunity to impress upon the community his political beliefs. Moreover, not only were doctrinal and political sermons heard from the pulpit, but also bits of important letters, decisions of ecclesiastical councils, proclamations from the seat of government, news from the army.[10]

Therefore, sermons often assumed the character of the basic information that the colonists would receive and, as such, they were well attended. "Except for quarterly town meetings," Kenneth Woodward notes in *Newsweek*, "sermons provided the only occasion when the entire community gathered. And they accompanied every public event: election days, thanksgiving days, funerals and military exercises. Whenever preachers had something to say, they would announce a fast day: all work ceased while the entire community assembled, often for as long as two hours at a stretch, to be reminded of their unique corporate identity as God's 'New Israel' and of their obligation to maintain a society worthy of his covenant."[11]

In the larger towns there was also a weekly lecture, less religious in character, at which a sermon was preached, and in the chief cities there had long been special occasions which gave the clergy opportunities to present their ideas before the public. There was the general election day, coming always in the spring, when the local governing body was elected. For this occasion, a special minister was chosen to preach the sermon which was, as a rule, printed by order of the colonial assembly and distributed. Usually one copy was distributed to each member of the assembly (legislature) and sometimes at least one or more to the minister or ministers of the towns.

Some of the election sermons discussed the government of the ancient Hebrews and its virtues. Many were theoretical, concerned with the origin and end of government. Some dealt more particularly with their own charters (constitutions) and the rights of Englishmen. Some, with great freedom of speech, gave practical advice to the government officials about well-known "evils" and desirable laws. The majority discussed in greater or less detail the qualities and responsibilities of government officials. "Year after year the same themes were discussed; often the same phraseology was used. Usually enough of the writer's own attitude appears to enable the reader to judge of his own conservatism or liberalism. Now and again there was an election preacher who was exceptionally direct and thoroughgoing in his discussion either of government or of the agitations of the day, or of both."[12]

One fact emerges clearly here. For a hundred years before the Revolution and year by year throughout the long conflict with Great Britain, these sermons dealt with matters of government and the people's relation to the government. They were heard by large audiences of clergy and laymen. They had the prestige of well-known names and of the colonial assembly attached to them. They were sent to friends in other colonies and in England. They were distributed regularly to the country towns where they became "text-books of politics."[13]

These sermons were printed and passed from hand to hand and from colony to colony in the thousands. The theories of these printed sermons reached the ears and eyes of the people of the colonies. As Stout has documented:

Twice on Sunday and often once during the week, every minister in New England delivered sermons lasting between one and two hours in length. Collectively over the entire span of the colonial period, sermons totaled over *five million separate messages* in a society whose population never exceeded one-half million and whose principal city never grew beyond seventeen thousand. The average weekly churchgoer in New England (and there were far more churchgoers than church members) listened to something like *seven thousand sermons* in a lifetime, totaling somewhere around *fifteen thousand hours of concentrated listening.*[14]

These striking statistics become even more significant when it is recalled that until the last decade of the colonial era there were at the local level few, if any, competing public speakers offering alternative messages. "For all intents and purposes, the sermon was the only regular voice of authority."[15]

However, it was not only the printed sermons which had an effect on the colonial mind. In fact, "[u]npublished regular sermons were more 'public' communications than their printed counterparts. Not everyone in New England *read* sermons, certainly not routinely, but nearly everyone *heard* them, week in, week out."[16]

These widely read and heard sermons had a great impact upon the people of the colonies. As the renowned Jonathan Mayhew commented, "The common people of New England, by means of our schools, and the instructions of our 'able, learned, orthodox ministers,' are, and have all along been, philosophers and divines in comparison of the common people in England, of the communion of the church there established. This is commonly said by those who have had an opportunity personally to inform themselves."[17]

THE FUSION OF RELIGIOUS AND POLITICAL CREEDS

In the sermons and related religious writings of the day, one finds striking analogies between religious and political creeds. Indeed, as one studies the everyday literature of the time, it becomes increasingly evident that the New England ideas of government were intimately connected with the interpretation of the Bible:

> The most common source was the Bible. The Old Testament furnished many illustrations of covenant relations, of the limitations placed upon rulers and people, of natural rights, of the divine constitution, etc. The New Testament gave authority for the liberties of Christians, for the relation of Christians to those in authority over them, and for the right of resistance. Indeed, there was never a principle derived from more secular reading that was not strengthened and sanctified by the Scriptures.[18]

If we are to attain any sort of reality concerning the developing colonial mind, we must recognize the enduring hold of the concept of *sola scriptura* (Scriptures only). Moreover, the "implications of enduring spirituality in the pulpit and pew are especially important for understanding the 'meaning of America' [or for that matter, the American dream] as it unfolded in the Revolutionary era. By 1776, Congregational ministers in New England were delivering over two thousand discourses a week and publishing them at an unprecedented rate that outnumbered secular pamphlets (from all the colonies) by a ratio of more than four to one."[19] And these pamphlets stood firm on the teachings of the Bible as they related to virtually all areas of life.

There were, of course, other sources that affected the thinking of the clergy. One such source was the writers of classical and late Roman days. The next great sources were the works of John Locke and Baron de Montesquieu. The writings of John Locke, his essays on religious toleration and human understanding as well as those on government, were influential on the thinking of the clergy. Some recent historians deemphasize the influence of Locke on colonial thinking,[20] but it is evident that he was quoted by name by the clergy and other colonial thinkers well before 1776. Moreover, his influence is seen in early colonial works. Especially after 1763 the references to him are numerous, not only by the more prominent ministers of the larger towns, but by those of the country villages as well.[21] "And in many works in which no direct reference is made one finds his theories, sometimes his very phrases, and this is true for years before 1761 as well as afterwards."[22]

Other writers who influenced the clergy included Martin Luther (1483-1546), John Calvin (1509-1564), Lord Edward Coke, John Milton, and others. Moreover, the ministers frequently quoted early election sermons, not only their own election sermons but the sermons by others, in their sermons, pamphlets, letters, and newspaper articles.

Again, these ministers were educated men. They had attended seminaries such as Harvard and Yale which emphasized the reading of the classics and other books which most contemporary seminaries would consider to be outside the realm of "religious" readings. For example:

Azariah Mather of Haddam in his Connecticut Election Sermon of 1725 referred to "Famous Bolton," Seneca, and Aesop. He quoted from Fuller: "A good Ruler is one that looks on Salus Populi to be Maxima Charta"; from Cicero: "Salus

Populi est Finis and imperii"; and from Henry: "Good Rulers will be in Pain, when Subjects are in Tears."[23]

Other sermons include references to and quotations from Jerome, Tertullian, Locke, Hoadly, Voltaire, Milton, and others.[24] As mentioned earlier, the clergy, as well as other colonial thinkers, practiced a pragmatism that allowed them to draw from varying materials to support their arguments, without denying the truths of the Bible (as they understood such truths).

Illustrations might be multiplied, but enough have been given to show something of the extent and variety of the sources from which the ministers drew their theories. However, "[i]t must not be forgotten," says Alice Baldwin, "in the multiplicity of the authors mentioned, that the source of greatest authority and the one most commonly used was the Bible."[25]

The New England preacher drew his beliefs largely from the Bible, which was to him a sacred book, infallible, "God's will for man":

> Of necessity it [the Bible] colored his political thinking. His conception of God, of God's law, and of God's relation to man determined to a large extent his conception of human law and of man's relation to his fellows. If his ideas of government and the rights of man were in part derived from other sources, they were strengthened and sanctioned by Holy Writ. This was of course especially true of the clergy. They stood before the people as interpreters of God's will. Their political speeches were sermons, their political slogans were often Bible texts. What they taught of government had about it the authority of the divine.[26]

Therefore, as Stout recognizes, the "more one reads these sermons the more one finds unsatisfactorily the suggestion that ideas of secular 'republicanism,' 'civil millennialism,' or class-conscious 'popular ideology' were the primary ideological triggers of radical resistance and violence in the Revolution. Such temporal concerns may have motivated other colonists, and they certainly engaged 'Americans' after 1776, but they were not the ideological core around which the Revolution in New England revolved. In Revolutionary New England, ministers continued to monopolize communications, and the terms they most often employed to justify resistance and to instill hope emanated from the Scriptures."[27]

To understand, however, something of the source and strength of the total political faith of colonial Americans, it is important that those views outside the confines of the Bible that influenced the clergy be discussed in some detail. These were writers that carried with them both Reformation and Enlightenment concepts.

F O U R

LOCKE

"*I*f we ask what book was most frequently cited by
Americans during the founding era," writes Professor Donald Lutz, "the answer somewhat surprisingly is: the Book of
Deuteronomy."[1] Moreover, as we have seen, the clergy and other
colonial leaders cited a number of varied writers in propounding
their politico-religious ideas to the people.

THE PURITANS

The striking feature of the religious makeup of seventeenth- and
eighteenth-century America is the preponderance of Calvinist
and neo-Calvinist thinking present in the clergy. This stems not
only from the predominance of Congregationalists and Presbyterians present in the colonies, but also because of the strong
Puritan influence still felt in New England. The Puritans were
heavily influenced by Calvinistic theology.

Concerning the Puritans, much "of what they said explicitly,
other Protestants of the seventeenth century shared implicitly;
but the Puritans' articulations gave the ideas distinct shape, both
intellectually and institutionally."[2] At least partially for such reasons, as Mark Noll, Nathan Hatch, and George Marsden write,
Puritan conceptions long remained major influences in America:

In most influential American churches Puritan categories
were commonplace until the mid-nineteenth century. Except
for a number of remarkable southern politicians, almost every prominent American thinker before World War I was
either born in New England or educated there. As late as the
early decades of the twentieth century many American liter-

ary figures were still wrestling with the vestiges of the Puritan heritage. And even more pervasive than such influences on American ideas was the Puritan impact on American values. While Puritanism could not claim to have single-handedly shaped the American conscience, it certainly helped define its most distinctive traits.[3]

The influence of religion on government has always been profound. It is no less true of Puritanism. Historian Clinton Rossiter writes that the "Puritan way of life is an earnest reminder that religion, especially the Christian religion as it emerged from the magnificent mind of John Calvin, was the ascendant element in the working philosophies of most colonists."[4] Again, it must be emphasized that John Calvin's philosophy was only one strong influence, among others, that affected the colonial mind.

Puritanism, as it relied on Calvinistic teachings, was a way of life which in its prime was an extension of a system of theology that held to the austere doctrines of an omnipotent God who intervenes constantly in the unfolding of nature and the lives of men. It speaks to corrupt and depraved men, for whom salvation through grace was the only need and goal; and that salvation came only through God's predestinating finger in selecting His elect to rule on earth. Also, Puritanism held that knowledge, true knowledge, was a gift of God to be received through revelation of the Bible rather than reason. However, as Rossiter notes: "The triumph of orthodox Puritanism as a theology was the signal of its failure as a way of life. It embraced too much, it dug too deep, it speculated too minutely. Most important, it made too much of piety among a people quite unready to renounce the world. Yet, 'reconstructed Puritanism,' the less austere but highly moralistic brand that developed in the colonies, was a leading way of life in eighteenth-century America."[5]

The Puritans viewed New England's corporate mission as recapitulating the mission of the Old Testament nation of Israel. Israel's experience as recounted in the Old Testament was, the Puritans believed, "a 'type' or model for their own experience as God's 'New Israel.' "[6] The related conclusion that America was chosen by God and destined to lead mankind has been traced by many historians to American Puritan concerns with the covenant and the millennium. And this millenarian vision eventually be-

came an essential ingredient of the American dream in terms of future optimism.

The continuing American moral fervor has, likewise, been traced to Puritan origins. Beyond this, the connection between the "spirit of capitalism" and the Protestant ethic can readily be illustrated in a New England line of descent from Cotton Mather (1663-1728) to Benjamin Franklin. Historian Sydney Ahlstrom emphasizes the "dominance of Puritanism in American religious heritage":

> [T]he future of the United States was settled and to a large degree shaped by those who brought with them a very special form of radical Protestantism which combined a strenuous moral precisionism, a deep commitment to evangelical experimentalism, and a determination to make the state responsible for the support of these moral and religious ideas. The United States became, therefore, the land *par excellence* of revivalism, moral "legalism" and a "gospel" of work that was undergirded by the so-called Puritan Ethic.[7]

The Puritans were not without their problems. There was a negative, intolerant side of Puritanism which they directed not only against nonbelievers but also against other non-Puritan Christians such as Catholics and Quakers. Unfortunately, many writers, by concentrating so heavily on Puritan rigidity and intolerance, have downplayed the legitimate and lasting contribution of Puritanism to American life. There is even a word—"puritanical"—that sums up this viewpoint. But if we dismiss Puritanism because of its defects, we cannot properly understand the American experience.

"Whatever of good and evil we owe" to the Puritans, writes Clinton Rossiter, "we owe their system some of the toughest elements of our constitutional democracy."[8] In fact, the cause of liberty and self-government in colonial America was nourished by several Puritan principles.

First, the Puritan concept of the covenant helped swell the triumph of the "dominant notion of eighteenth-century popularism, the social contract."[9] The Puritans were, as Perry Miller and others have demonstrated, obsessed with the covenant or contract, relying on it to explain almost every relation of man to man and man to God:[10]

Of the seven or eight covenants recognized in orthodox Puritanism, the church covenant was the particular forerunner of the eighteenth-century contract. The Puritan theory of the origin of the church in the consent of the believers led directly to the popular theory of the origin of government in the consent of the governed. The doctrines of popular government held in many a Massachusetts village were largely a secularized and expanded Congregationalism.[11]

And as Harry Stout recognizes:

Covenant theology as it evolved over five generations of New World preaching comprised a view of history and corporate identity that could best be labeled "providential." In this view God entered into covenants with nations, as well as with individuals, and promised that he would uphold them by his providential might if they would acknowledge no other sovereign and observe the terms of obedience contained in his Word. Covenanted peoples like those of ancient Israel and New England were the hub around which sacred (i.e., real) history revolved. Such peoples might be ignored or reviled by the world and figure insignificantly in the great empires of profane history, but viewed through the sacred lens of providential history they were seen as God's special instruments entrusted with the task of preparing the way for messianic deliverance. As Israel witnessed to God's active involvement with nations in ancient times and brought forth the Christ, so New England's experience confirmed God's continuing involvement with nations that would persist until Christ's return to earth, when history itself would cease and be swallowed up in eternity.[12]

Within this historical perspective, "resistance to England was only secondarily about constitutional rights and political liberties. Ultimately, resistance became necessary the minute England declared the colonies' duty of 'unlimited submission' in 'all cases whatsoever' and, in so doing, set itself alongside God's Word as a competing sovereign."[13] Such demands were "tyrannical" and left New Englanders no choice but to resist unto death or forfeit their identity as a covenant people. As explained from the pulpit, revolution was first and foremost a battle to preserve their histor-

ic identity and unique messianic destiny. In light of the emphasis on covenantal concerns, it is hardly accidental, then, that "New England ministers gave the first and most cordial reception to the arguments of John Locke and other great English liberals, and broadcast from their pulpits the new gospel of government by consent."[14]

Second, the Puritans were firm believers in higher law. They did not, however, imagine a higher law in any nebulous sense. Instead, they were able to point to its existence in writing. It was their conviction—and here they broke sharply with the mother church in England—"that the Scriptures offered correct answers to all problems of individual conduct, church government, and social and political organization":

> Although the Puritan determination to adhere rigidly to Hebraic mandates weakened and gave way under the stresses of human nature and the American environment, the belief in higher law—law that could be appealed to against the arbitrariness of rulers—carried over irresistibly into the developing American creed. The law of nature, like the social contract, got an especially warm reception among descendants of Puritans. And the traditional American insistence on a written constitution owes something to the insistence of the Puritan that higher law could be written law.[15]

A third contribution of Puritanism to liberty was the substance it gave to the doctrine of individualism (within moral constraints). It may be strange to think of Puritanism, with its concepts of human depravity, predestination, and political authoritarianism, as a wellspring of eighteenth-century as well as modern individualism. However, as Rossiter writes:

> Yet under this cruel exterior lurked notions of a liberating character, and these were to emerge in good season as a rich inheritance for American democracy. Even the most rigidly orthodox Puritans betrayed suspicions that man was somehow responsible, competent, and potentially decent; that his own interpretation of Scripture, not a priest's thirdhand account of revealed dogma, was to control his actions; that salvation was the result of an inner experience, not a conformity to certain modes of worship; and that the way to

eternity was open to all men without regard to political, economic, or social standing.[16]

Most important, as the eminent jurist Roscoe Pound has written: "Puritanism put individual judgment and individual conscience in the first place where the traditional modes of thought had put authority and the reason and judgment of the prince."[17] When challenging the claims of hierarchy the Puritans had to stress the competence of the individual, and in doing so they opened the door to religious and political equality. The uncompromising insistence of eighteenth-century liberal preachers on the "right of private judgment" was the "democratic fruit" of these seeds of orthodox Puritanism.[18]

Economic individualism—a dominant feature of the American model of political democracy—also owes a debt to Puritanism. Government regulation of the economy was an accepted part of the Puritans' scheme of things. However, by insisting that a sober and godly life was both a sign of salvation and a path to prosperity, by sanctifying the virtues of industry, frugality, and self-reliance, the Puritans "helped create a collective state of mind and morality that would make possible the rise of American capitalism. American democracy has been, in the best and truest sense of the terms, middle-class, bourgeois, free-enterprise democracy, and Puritanism did as much as any other 'way of life' to give our democracy the special flavor. Puritanism was not free enterprise, but some of the best Puritans were conscious free-enterprisers."[19]

A fifth key source of the American belief in the dependence of liberty on an educated citizenry was the Puritan emphasis on general education. Although some prominent early colonials, such as Roger Williams (1603-1685), simply ignored the problem of education, it was the much maligned Puritan of Massachusetts and Connecticut—the man who insisted on a learned ministry, "enlightened" saints, and common men at least able to read the Bible—who first showed faith in the efficacy of education. "The instruments of education erected by the early New England Puritans in the face of overwhelming odds were not designed to further liberty as we understand it. Yet these instruments and the philosophy that sustained them were to prove readily convertible to the broader, more humane uses of later generations."[20] The Puritans, in founding such institutions as

Harvard College, gave birth to a form of higher education that predominates even to this present day.

Moreover, the Puritan emphasis on education remained strong up through the Revolutionary War and well beyond. Even into the nineteenth century, religion and education were closely associated in the American mind.[21] As it was with the Puritans, colonial education's "chief purpose was to support revealed religion."[22] This fact continued to influence even the fundamentally skeptical such as Benjamin Franklin, who considered the inculcation of Christian ethics to be the common element of education for every class and the marrow of education.

Finally, it must never be forgotten, especially in an age of upheaval and disillusionment, that American democracy rests squarely on the assumption of a pious, honest, self-disciplined, moral people. For all its faults and falterings, for all the distance it has yet to travel, "American democracy has been and remains a highly *moral* adventure."[23] Whatever doubts may exist about the sources of this democracy, there can be none about the chief source of the morality that gives it life and substance.

> From Puritanism, from the way of life that exalted individual responsibility, came those homely rules of everyday conduct—or, if we must, those rationalizations of worldly success—that have molded the American mind into its unique shape. Puritanism was the goad to the American conscience that insisted on communal responsibility before individual freedom, constitutionalism before democracy, order before liberty. If democracy has flourished in these states as strongly as anywhere in the world, it is because we are drawing still upon the moral vigor of Puritanism.[24]

Probably the greatest influence that the Puritans had on the American culture was their embracing of the doctrines of Calvinism and then transforming them to a politico-religious philosophy. As a consequence, New England society and clergy both were steeped in Calvinistic political ideas. This opened the door for the European thinkers who had been influenced by Calvinistic political doctrines, such as John Locke, who transmitted the basic ideas that were later to be formulated in the Declaration of Independence and were to constitute the fabric of the American dream.

MR. LOCKE

The writings of the English political thinker John Locke greatly influenced the colonial clergy. Especially in the first part of the eighteenth century, Locke's thought helped formulate the basic political philosophy of the American clergy and, through the clergy, that of the colonial people.

Locke was brought up by a Puritan father.[25] Historian John Dunn writes:

> Lockean social and political theory is to be seen as the elaboration of Calvinist social values, in the absence of a terrestrial focus of theological authority and in response to a series of particular challenges. The explanation why it was *Calvinist* social values which Locke continued to expound is that he was brought up in a Calvinist family. And the reason why he *continued* to expound them is that his own experience was too dominated by "uneasiness," too anxious, to make a self-confident naturalism a tolerable interpretation of the world. . . . His own psychology and his own biography conspired to retain him within the inherited theological framework and in consequence the honesty and force of his thought were devoted to making such sense as could be made of this framework instead of to replacing it.[26]

Some have questioned the orthodoxy of Locke's Christian beliefs. It is true that Locke did not hold what most would term a distinctly Christian world view. In fact, as a purported Christian, he did not realize that the implications of his thinking would eventually "secularize" certain Christian doctrines. Moreover, those who argue that many of Locke's beliefs led to modern secular rationalism are probably correct.[27]

However, whether or not Locke was an entirely orthodox Christian is beside the point. The fact is that Lockean philosophy, by the way of the clergy and other leaders, had a significant impact on the colonial American mind. Reformation thinking and the diluted doctrines of a political Calvinism were conveyed to the colonial mind partly—though by no means exclusively—through "John Locke's *Second Treatise on Civil Government*, which appeared in 1690."[28] There is some dispute in academia concerning which works of Locke influenced colonial Americans.[29] What is more important, however, is that gen-

erally his treatment of such subjects as natural law and natural rights reduces almost completely into life, liberty, and resistance.[30]

Finally, we must remember that people are often products of the thinking of the times in which they live. This was no less true of John Locke. He lived in an age when rationalism and empiricism were emerging with great force, and these, naturally, affected his Christian frame of mind.

LOCKE'S THINKING

Locke's political theory, concisely stated, held that government exists by the consent of the governed, and therefore a ruler who loses the confidence of the people no longer has the right to govern them. Locke articulated this theory in his *Two Treatises of Civil Government* as an attempt to justify the English Revolution of 1688 by refuting two popularly held theories: the "divine right" of kings and the absolute power of kings.

Locke's political theory, although influenced by his Christianity, rested largely upon rationalism and the idea that proper regulation of society requires an understanding of the prior "state of nature" from which civil society developed. Locke explained such development in terms of a theoretical "contract" which induced men to leave the state of nature and enter the political society.[31] It is here that the obvious influence of the Calvinistic emphasis on the covenant (contract) is apparent. However, the question inevitably emerged: Who are "the people," and how did they become an entity capable of contracting? Locke's own answer to these questions springs from three basic sources.

First, there was the English legal tradition as illustrated in Sir Edward Coke (1552-1634) and others, the primary emphasis of which has always been on the rights of the individual rather than on rights of people collectively.[32] Second, Locke himself would have been the first to acknowledge his indebtedness to European and classical thinkers such as Hugo Grotius (1583-1645), Issac Newton (1642-1727), Cicero (106-43 B.C.), and so on.[33] Finally, a source was "English Independency," which was in turn the direct outgrowth of Martin Luther's doctrine of the priesthood of the individual believer.[34] As professor Edward Corwin has recognized: "For in a period in which religious and political controversy were so closely involved with each other as in seven-

teenth-century England, ideas developed in one forum were easily and inevitably transferred to the other."[35]

It is at this point that Locke's Christian heritage had a direct impact on the development of his political doctrine. The concept of the priesthood of the individual led to the belief that individuals possess rights independent of institutions such as church and state. Luther summed it up thusly:

> Since we are all priests and all have one faith, one gospel, and one sacrament, why then should we not have the authority to test and determine what is right in the faith? Abraham had to listen to Sarah who was more subject than we are to anyone on earth, and Balaam's ass was wiser than the prophet himself. If then God could speak through an ass against a prophet, then can he not speak through a godly man against the pope? . . . Therefore it behooves every Christian to espouse the cause of the faith, to understand and defend it, and to rebuke all errors.[36]

The priesthood of individuals—that is, the right of the individual to stand in judgment over established authorities including government—as promulgated through Locke and other European writers and the Puritans and as translated through the colonial clergy became a bedrock of liberty. As Rossiter writes:

> American democracy owes its greatest debt to colonial Protestantism for the momentum it gave to the growth of individualism. The Reformation, which was powered by the revolutionary notion that man could commune with God without the intercession of a priest, did as much as the rise of capitalism to spread the doctrine of individualism. As the Protestants of Protestantism, the dissidents of dissent, the American churches stressed the salvation of the individual rather than the maintenance of communal unity or doctrinal purity. Calvinist in inspiration and Puritan in essence, the great dissenting churches helped breed a new person, and this man, multiplied millions of times over, was to give American democracy its peculiar flavor. In its best aspects and moments Protestantism was a main source of these great political principles of American democracy: freedom of thought and expression, separation of church and state, local self-government, higher law, constitutionalism, the American Mission, and the free individual.[37]

Locke, then, accumulated the ideas of many and collated them in his writings. As a politico-religious doctrine, they had a lasting impact and were a basis of the American Revolution.

THE STATE OF NATURE

Locke postulated that there was a state of nature. In nature, people live together according to reason, with no commonly acknowledged superior having the authority to judge between them. Thus, all people are equal and independent.

Locke depicted the state of nature as a condition of peace, goodwill, mutual assistance, and preservation in which the free, "sovereign" individual is already in possession of all valuable rights, though from defect of "executive power" the individual is not always able to make them good or to determine them accurately in relation to the like rights of his fellows.[38] And from this difference flow all the others. As such, society existed before all government. In this respect, Locke regarded government as creative of no rights, but as strictly fiduciary in character, and as designed to make more secure and more readily available rights which antedate it and which would survive it.

Within this state of nature, everyone possesses "natural rights" to life, liberty, and property. The right to life is a right of self-preservation. Liberty is the right to do as one pleases without violating the equal rights of others. The right to property derives from the right to one's labor and the fruits thereof.

Second, man has a fundamentally social character, by necessity, convenience, and inclination. Third, there is a "law of nature" which is morally binding on everyone, even in the absence of governmental enforcement. With Locke, natural law approximates to positive (written) law; and even after the establishment of civil government, popular interpretation of natural law is the ultimate test of the validity of civil law.

Three important institutions exist in the state of nature: property, money, and family. Private property comes into being whenever labor is applied to free goods. The things of earth, in their natural form, belong to everyone. Once labor is applied, however, goods become the property of the laborer, since everyone is entitled to his own labor and the fruits thereof. As a corollary, those who do not labor are not entitled to own property. Yet the hoarding of perishable goods is wrong, and any unused, rotting, or perishing goods may justifiably be taken by others.

Money is any lasting thing that may be kept without spoiling and that by mutual consent men would take in exchange for truly useful but perishable necessities. Production of surplus perishable goods creates a need for exchange. The accumulation of imperishable goods helps to serve this purpose. Such "hoarding" is justified because there is no unnecessary waste or spoilage.

Family, the inevitable outcome of man's social nature, is a voluntary contract that is morally binding without enforcement. In matters of common interest, the husband controls. Both husband and wife have authority over children, with a corresponding obligation to serve them. The wife retains her peculiar rights by contract.

The state of nature is not the perfectly ideal state, because it leads invariably to a "state of war," which is any invasion of the natural rights of others. Liberty in the hands of some people degenerates into uncontrolled license, which requires others to take up the defense of their natural rights. The result is an endless struggle and a need for incessant precaution.

The state of war in turn may lead to the existence of slavery. Since no one has a right over his own life, voluntary slavery is morally impermissible. But one who invades the rights of others forfeits his own rights and may be pressed into slavery. This slavery is not absolute, however, and the master is not entitled to possession of the slave's property beyond what is needed to make restitution.

Dissatisfaction with the state of nature induced men to form political society. They were willing to surrender a portion of their individual freedom to unite with others for the mutual preservation of their natural rights. Men can settle disputes in an orderly, peaceful fashion only by appeal to a common authority under whom all have agreed to live. The only way to avoid the state of war is to enforce the law of nature by social contract or *covenant*.

THE POLITICAL SOCIETY

The political society is inherently superior to the state of nature, which lacks three important elements: a set of universally accepted laws, an indifferent judge or judges to settle disputes, and the power to enforce and execute penalties. The political society provides these elements in the form of the legislative, judicial, and executive powers. The chief end of government is *negative,* in the sense of protecting natural rights by restraining men from doing wrong, rather than seeking to secure affirmative goods for society. Thus, government should not be involved in personal affairs, such as family and church.

All legitimate governments rest on the consent of the governed. Rulers who have not been freely chosen by the people are illegitimate and have no right of obedience from the people.

This concept, however, raises two problems. Since all people do not have the same opinions and desires, unanimity is impracticable. Some people will not give their consent. Yet the majority has the power of the whole, by the law of nature and by reason, and may exercise power over the minority. Such a society still renders benefits to those in the minority and is, therefore, superior to the state of nature.

Another problem is that most people grow up as citizens of pre-existing states without an opportunity to form their own government. However, children who enter their parents' political group may be presumed to have given tacit consent to the social contract. Children who assert their freedom (after reaching maturity) may withdraw their loyalty and enter another political state of their choosing, subject to the following constraints. As long as they remain in their parents' state, they must obey the laws established by their parents. The underlying assumption is that everyone is born free, a subject of no government, and remains free to choose his own political allegiance. However, once chosen, he or she is subject to that allegiance unless the government violates the rights to life, liberty, and property.

Of all the types of governments, Locke argued that democracy is the best and the safest against tyranny. Since the legislative power is supreme, governments may be classified by the way they allocate that power. In a monarchy, the legislative power is vested in one ruler. In an oligarchy, it is vested in a select few. Only in a democracy is the legislative power vested in all citizens.

Although hereditary monarchy was the earliest political form, it is inferior because it eventually degenerates and produces unacceptable rulers. Hereditary oligarchy creates an aristocracy whose members are too easily tempted to rule for selfish advantage. The only safe form of government is democracy, with a legislative assembly composed of elected delegates serving limited terms, subject to dismissal and succession by others.

Only this form allows citizens to remove bad or ineffective rulers.

Locke, probably because of his English background, preferred to retain the hereditary kingship as a "limited monarchy," with executive but not legislative power. That power theoretically derives from the consent of the people and is held only as long as the king rules with wisdom and justice. In some cases, the king's executive power is superior to legislative power. The king may withhold his consent on certain bills. He may exercise legislative power when the legislature is not in session. He may exercise arbitrary authority in time of pressing emergency. Finally, he may at times assemble, refuse to assemble, or dismiss the legislature. But at all times the king remains subject to the law, and a king who attempts to rule in his own right acts as a single private person without power or right to obedience.

Two features of Locke's *Second Treatise* which have impressed themselves on American thinking are the limitations which it lays down for legislative power and its emphasis on the property right. The legislature is the supreme organ of Locke's commonwealth, and it is upon this supremacy that he depends in the main for the safeguarding of the rights of individuals. However, legislative supremacy is supremacy within the law, not power above the law. In fact, the word *sovereign* is never used by Locke in its descriptive sense except in reference to the "free, sovereign" individual in the state of nature.

Locke specifies the following limitations to legislative power. First, it is not arbitrary power. Not even the majority which determines the form of the government can vest its agent (the legislature) with arbitrary power. This is for the simple reason that the majority right itself originates in a delegation by free, sovereign individuals who had in the state of nature no arbitrary power over the life, liberty, possessions of others, or even over their own. In this *caveat* against arbitrary power, Locke definitely anticipates the modern concept of due process of law.

Second, the legislative power cannot assume to itself a power to rule by extemporary, arbitrary decrees, but is bound to dispense justice and decide the rights of the subject by promulgated standing laws and known authorized judges. Locke argues that to be effective, law must be general; it must afford equal protection to all; it may not validly operate retroactively; it must be enforced through the courts—that is, legislative power does not include judicial power.

Third, as also follows from its fiduciary character, the legislature cannot transfer the power of making laws to any other hands. This is because the legislature, being a delegated power from the people, cannot be passed to others. Thus, legislative power cannot be delegated.

Finally, legislative power is not the ultimate power of governments. The community perpetually retains a supreme power of saving themselves from the attempts and designs of anybody, "even the legislators, whenever they shall be so foolish or so wicked as to lay and carry on designs against the liberties and properties of the subject."[39]

THE RIGHT OF REVOLUTION

In case the political system fails, the law of nature still binds society, and there may a "right of revolution." Revolution is morally permissible whenever the king exceeds the power conferred on him by the political contract. Specifically, the right of revolution pertains whenever the king establishes his own arbitrary will in place of the law; hinders the legislature from assembling; attempts to convene a legislature composed of his own "tools"; betrays his subjects to a foreign power; confiscates the property of his subjects; or violates the people's trust in any other way. Under such conditions, the king dissolves the government and ceases to be king.

Because possession of the power to rule does not automatically confer the right to rule, revolution is always permissible against absolute monarchs and usurpers. In Lockean terms, an absolute monarchy is not even a civil government. People cannot consent to a ruler's absolute power over their lives, because according to natural law no one has that power even over his own life. In addition, there is no neutral judge to decide between the monarch and the people, and thus an absolute monarchy is in essence a state of war. Likewise, a usurper destroys the political contract by depriving the people of their right to choose their own ruler.

There may even be a right of revolution against the legislature if it exceeds its powers and attempts to rule for private advantage. For instance, if the legislature grasps arbitrary power, invades the people's property rights, delegates its own power to others, or refuses to proclaim fixed laws, it ceases to be the legislature, loses its supreme power under the contract (or constitution), and declares a "state of war." At that point, the people are freed from their obligation to the government. They may revolt (or resist) and form a new government.

The right of revolution, however, is not unlimited. The people must always uphold their end of the political contract. Three factors must be present to justify a revolution. The people must be assailed by an unjust and unlawful force. There must be no opportunity to appeal to a neutral tribunal according to legal process (or no such tribunal in existence). And a majority of the people must agree to cooperate in the revolution. As such, it is never appropriate for a minority of people to disturb the peace by resisting the government.

In any case, dissolution of the government does not mean the dissolution of society. The breakup of political society returns everyone to his previous state, with the individual liberty to shift allegiance to other societies. For a time this may result in a confused multitude, without order or connection. But society is preserved by the social inclination of man. The law of nature still holds, and everyone retains complete freedom and natural rights. The lack of political protection, coupled with the desire to avoid a state of war, will inevitably bring a transition to a new political contract.

LOCKEAN REFLECTION IN AMERICAN REVOLUTION
It is obvious from even a casual reading of John Locke that the American colonists adopted, at least in part, what could be termed a Lockean view of rights and resistance. This philosophy is enunciated in the Declaration of Independence and was applied in the American Revolution. It was likewise espoused by the American clergy long before 1776.

As previously noted, however, Locke was expounding a philosophy he inherited from the European Reformation and which was colored by Enlightenment thinking. At core, it had roots in what has been termed "political Calvinism." It was also an expansion and application of principles disseminated in the resistance writings of the sixteenth century.

THE GROUNDS FOR REVOLUTION

Shortly after the publication in 1690 of John Locke's *Two Treatises of Government,* one observer noted: "Locke's Civil Government proves that the sovereignty belongs to the people. . . . This is the gospel of the day among Protestants."[1] Some seventy years later, during the American Revolution, another remarked: "The Americans have made the maxims of Locke the ground of the present war."[2]

Locke, as well as other thinkers, was, so to speak, common property on the eve of the American Revolution. He was quoted in its defense by "James Otis, John Adams, Sam Adams, and the Boston town meeting, the Massachusetts assembly, Revolutionary preachers—Howard, West, Stillman, Haven, Whitaker; owned and studied by Jonathan Mayhew; read and recommended by Hamilton, Franklin, and Jefferson; and incorporated in the Declaration of Independence."[3] In other words, Lockean philosophy was an important element in what Thomas Jefferson termed "the American mind."

However, as with all philosophers, Locke's philosophy was intertwined with his heritage and the thinkers who preceded him. Moreover, his Calvinistic background logically led him to espouse a certain politico-religious doctrine.

POLITICAL CALVINISM

Michael Walzer in his book *The Revolution of the Saints* writes: "Calvinistic saintliness, after all, has scarred us all, leaving its mark if not on our conscious then on our clandestine minds. . . . The Calvinist saint seems to me now the first of those self-disciplined agents of social and political reconstruction who have appeared so frequently in modern history. He is the destroyer of an old order for which there is no need to feel nostalgic. . . . He is, above all, an extraordinarily bold, inventive, and ruthless politician, as a man should be who has 'great works' to perform, as a man, perhaps, must be, for 'great works have great enemies.' "[4]

The European Calvinism of the sixteenth and seventeenth centuries, through its resistance writings, was one such work that formed "great enemies." As it was blended into a coherent politico-religious doctrine, it became an effective tool for the call for liberty, resistance, and the rights of man.

Locke, as we saw, was influenced by a form of Calvinism which he mixed with rationalism and certain Christian beliefs. This doctrine, which was grasped by American colonial leadership, was a peculiar type of philosophical persuasion.

Locke's philosophy was obviously derived from those whom he had studied. He cites authorities sparingly, but as Herbert D. Foster documents, in "his *Two Treatises on Government* his citations are almost entirely Calvinistic: Scripture seventy-nine times; seven Calvinists (Hooker, Bilson, James I., Milton, Hunton, Ainsworth, Selden); one ex-Calvinist, the Dutch Remonstrant Grotius; and only one reference uninfected by Calvinism, the Scottish Catholic Barclay."[5]

In his political theories, Locke epitomized the five points of what has been called "political Calvinism."[6] Labels are often misleading, but Locke could be called an Anglo-Calvinist, or better, an "international Calvinist."[7]

However, it "is true he was not of the narrower, scholastic seventeenth-century Calvinists, but rather he imbibed and passed on the moderate liberal Calvinism of the earlier unembittered Calvin and the sixteenth-century creeds, preserved by Huguenots, Independents, sixteenth-century Dutch and Anglicans, and early Remonstrants."[8] What this means is that political Calvinism is not equivalent to the religious doctrines that are usually associated with the "narrower" Calvinism. Thus, political Calvinism, in the end, has little to do with predestination, total depravity, and the like. Political Calvinism, then, is what the name implies—a political doctrine derived from religious roots.

This was what Locke was asserting in his writings and this is where he had his great impact, especially in America. As Foster argues: "Through Locke there filtered to the American Revolution five points of political Calvinism held by hundreds of Calvinists, but clarified through his *Civil Government:* fundamental law, natural rights, contract and consent of people, popular sovereignty, resistance to tyranny through responsible representatives."[9] Again, these tenets were not the sole foundations for the American Revolution but did exert a strong influence.

FUNDAMENTAL LAW

The first point of political Calvinism is fundamental law. Foster writes:

> From the absolute sovereignty of God and the authority of his Word, Calvin's successor Beza deduced the conclusion of "no other will which is perpetual and immutable, the rule of justice." "God only hath this prerogative: whose sovereignty is absolute, and whose will is a perfect Rule and Reason itself," argued Governor John Winthrop. Baxter reasoned that "God as the sovereign ruler of Mankind hath given him the Law of Nature, commonly called the Moral Law." The Huguenot *Vindiciae contra Tyrannos* calls it the "Law of God." Calvin's dictum, "the written law is nothing but the corroboration of the law of nature," represents the general Calvinist tendency to identify the law of nature with the law of God, though not with the Old Testament. Calvin, Ponet, the Genevan Version of the Bible, Hotman, Pareus, Junius, Buchanan, Lilburne, and Locke taught that the law of nature was "corroborated," "contained," or "summarized" in that part of Moses's law which was fundamental and moral, not ceremonial.[10]

Fundamental law is called "the law of God and Nature" by a number of early writers. This fundamental law sometimes appears as simply the "law of nature" in Calvin, Locke, and others.[11] It is also the "law of reason" in both Calvin and Locke.[12]

The idea of a law of nature itself did not originate with the Calvinists. That the "Calvinists made no pretense of originating the idea of a law of nature"[13] is beside the point. The fact is that Locke believed in a fundamental "law of nature," "contained in the book of the law of Moses."[14] And this he passed on to posterity.

NATURAL RIGHTS

The existence of natural rights was the second tenet of political Calvinism. Rights, bestowed by God and based upon God's fundamental law of nature, are a part of both divine and human nature and, therefore, are natural and inalienable.

> Calvin in his Commentary on Romans (iii. 29) dropped fertile seeds. "God made the whole human race equal and placed them under one condition." "It is a law of nature that all men are formed in the image of God and are to be brought up in the hope of blessed eternity." Calvin's *Institutes* held "reason a natural talent," and on the basis of "the divine word and the experience of common sense" discovered God-given "principles of equity," "seeds of justice and also some seeds of political order sown in the minds of all," "some desire of investigating truth," and "making new discoveries," especially in "civil polity, domestic economy, all the mechanical arts and liberal sciences." . . . Such inspiring conceptions of human possibilities, sown by Calvin and ripened among Huguenots, Independents, Dutch, and Scots, came to fruition in Locke and America.[15]

That all men were created equal by natural law or the law of God was obviously taught by Calvin. That all men were born free was maintained by a number of Calvinists including the American Roger Williams, John Milton, as well as Locke himself.[16] Even the natural right of property had been taught by such Calvinists as Beza, Pareus, the Levellers, and others long before Locke was even born.[17]

Reason as a natural right had been taught before Locke by Calvin and those who adhered to Calvinistic political doctrines. In fact, one early Calvinist wrote: "Man is a rational creature, therefore the Prince must be subject to reason."[18] "Before Locke, practically all his natural rights of equality, liberty, life, property, conscience, and reason had been taught by Calvinists as corollaries of the fundamental law of God and nature which created man free, equal, and rational."[19]

CONTRACT AND CONSENT OF THE PEOPLE

The idea of "mutual relation" between God and man was implied in the Calvinists' thought of the "Word of God." They taught a like mutual relation between ruler and people. "Every commonwealth," said Calvin, "rests upon laws and agreements" and "the mutual obligations of head and members."[20] Foster notes:

> "Regal power was nothing but a mutual covenant between king and people," said the Scottish commissioners, justifying to Elizabeth their "demission" of Mary, and quoting Calvin's teaching. This contract idea, embodied by one of the commissioners, Buchanan, in his much-quoted book, passed on through his pupil, James I., who was quoted by Locke. Buchanan, Milton, Vane, Prynne, Baxter, Du Moulin, and John Cotton draw the logical conclusion that "the rights of him who dissolves the contract are forfeited."[21]

This doctrine of a mutual contract, the violation of which gave people or their representatives the right to resist the ruler, had been taught by over sixty Calvinists and successfully practiced by Calvinists in six countries before Locke popularized it in his writings.[22] In England, the contract theory was taught by Calvinists of all sorts, many of whom were cited in Locke's writings.[23]

Closely allied with the contract theory was the doctrine of the consent of the people, a theory sometimes passing imperceptibly into the "sovereignty of the people." The consent of the people was of extraordinary significance among Calvinists. Like the idea of the priesthood of the individual, it was applied to the church and was then extended to the state. Locke followed the footsteps of a dozen Calvinists, among whom were John Calvin himself, Thomas Hooker (1586-1647), John Cotton, Roger Williams, and others. The tendency of Calvinists to extend from church to state the consent of the people and ideas of republican government is corroborated by a score of scholarly critics.[24]

POPULAR SOVEREIGNTY

Believing that rulers receive their power by consent of the people, and could govern only when they observed their contract (covenant), the logically minded Calvinist was bound in time to take the next step and recognize the sovereignty of the people. Before Calvin's death, a number of Calvinists taught in books (published even at Geneva) that kings are "but a portion and a member of the people"; "people are not ordained for kings, but kings are ordained for the people" or "the whole Congregation or Commonwealth."[25] That "People were not made for kings but kings for the people" was a favorite Calvinist teaching, proclaimed by many Calvinists prior to Locke.[26] John Milton, like other Calvinists, taught that the people are the "proximate" or direct cause of sovereignty.[27] Locke repeats this teaching of over thirty international Calvinists, most of whose works he knew.[28]

RESISTANCE TO TYRANNY THROUGH RESPONSIBLE REPRESENTATIVES

The doctrine of resistance to tyranny through responsible representatives was taught early on in Calvin's *Institutes*.[29] It is also repeated by some twenty-eight Calvinists before Locke.[30] Calvin's teaching on resistance was cited by numerous Calvinist writers—including Samuel Rutherford (1600-1661) in *Lex Rex* in 1644.[31] One early Calvinist document, written in 1606, stated: "When any such new forms of government, begun by Rebellion, are after thoroughly settled, the authority in them is of God."[32] Foster writes:

> The Revolution of 1688 which Locke aided and justified, and his own teaching of resistance to tyranny through responsible representatives, which he based upon fundamental law, contract, natural rights, and the sovereignty of the people, were in the main historical outgrowths of international Calvinism. This is not to assert that no other elements entered into Locke or the Revolution. Calvinists did not claim to be original. They built upon the past; but they "took the next step," possibly the most distinguishing contribution of Calvinism. . . . With a possible exception on this point, the contribution of Calvinism was not in originating, but in (1) carrying theories to logical conclusions; (2) tying them all together in a workable system; (3) developing the type of people capable of putting them into practice; (4) demonstrating that their principles worked successfully in practice.[33]

VINDICIAE CONTRA TYRANNOS

An example of a Calvinist writing which influenced John Locke was the *Vindiciae contra Tyrannos* or *A Defense of Liberty Against Tyrants,* published in 1579.[34] In fact, it is difficult to overestimate the resemblance between the ideas of Locke and the author of the *Vindiciae*. Political historians have now carefully documented that Locke not only read the *Vindiciae*, but also listed it in his journals as an entry in his "Catalogue of My Books at Oxford."[35]

Protestantism by the midsixteenth century was undergoing a rigorous persecution from many different directions. One historian notes: "When Calvin died in 1564 the lines were already drawn for the religious wars which, as Luther had said, were to 'fill the world with blood.' "[36] In the Netherlands, for example, the Calvinists felt the stirring of their absentee "landlord," Philip II of Spain, who promised to obliterate the scourge of Protestantism (a promise embarked upon in Spain). Perhaps more significantly for resistance literature, the French Huguenots were caught in the middle of a series of civil wars (1562-1598) between the noble houses of Guise and Bourbon. No atrocity or persecution characterized the struggles nor depicted the Protestant plight as did the St. Bartholomew's Day Massacre of 1572.

The century between 1550 and 1650 saw the publication, translation, and reprinting of literally scores of resistance tracts and pamphlets.[37] As history illustrates, active resistance invariably follows the proliferation of resistance writings. This was true of European resistance movements of the sixteenth century, the American Revolution, and contemporary Christian activism.[38]

"Of all this rather numerous class of works, however, the most famous was the *Vindiciae contra Tyrannos*, published in 1579, which systematized the argument presented in the preceding few years."[39] While *Vindiciae* was the "greatest and undoubtedly the most famous contribution to the Huguenot theory of revolution,"[40] it was pseudonymously released under the name of Stephanus Junius Brutus. However, subsequent scholarship has attributed the tract to Philippe Du Plessis-Mornay (1549-1623), a counselor to Henry IV.[41]

Harold Laski notes: "Through Locke, also, it supplies the perspective of the American Revolution."[42] "Indeed the actual ideas of Du Plessis-Mornay are more completely realized in the American Constitution."[43]

The publication of the *Vindiciae*, of course, was labeled as heresy by the ruling forces. As one historian notes: "Often appealed to by those who would limit the powers of kings over the people, it is one of the most influential books in revolutionary literature. . . . That the book was publicly burned at Cambridge (1620) and at Oxford (1683) is an indication of the danger it was supposed to present to established authority."[44]

There are a number of political and social concepts which historians and political academicians have, at least in part, attributed to the *Vindiciae* and its author's fellow second-generation Reformation theorists. While many, if not all, of these concepts had been introduced and treated singularly at prior junctures in history in vastly different contexts, what is significant about their emergence in late-Reformation literature is that they were resurrected to create elements of a unified political theory which enjoyed mass following especially among the widely distributed and influential Calvinists. Moreover, the *Vindiciae's* ideas were also widely circulated and selectively adhered to by theorists such as John Locke. As a result, they later found their way across the Atlantic to the American colonies.

The specific theories represented in the *Vindiciae* which were to emerge with new emphasis in later political thought include the following:[45] supremacy of natural law;[46] law as the embodiment of reason, and thus free from human passions;[47] no man, royalty inclusive, is above the law;[48] popular sovereignty;[49] "popular sovereignty is . . . the basis of royal power";[50] man is free by nature and subjects himself to the king only under the condition that the monarch protects the general welfare;[51] the inference "that any legitimate political society must originate in an act of free consent on the part of the whole populace";[52] "the state is the result of a definite act of choice";[53] "the state as a human, even artificial, contrivance";[54] limited power (a concept "akin to that between the supporters of the Union and those of State rights in America");[55] "the contractual, and therefore limited, character of government";[56] the people swear a "conditional" obligation to the king while the king's obligation is "absolute";[57] any king who willfully violates the contract is a tyrant, and "the officers of the kingdom" are "empowered by their own right to drive him out";[58] "the power of representative assemblies is in fact 'ephoral' in character";[59] "the legal right of Parlements to act as a check on the king" or " 'judge between the king and the people.' "[60]

THE FOUR QUESTIONS
The author of the *Vindiciae* develops these principles within the context of four questions confronting the European Calvinists of

his time.[61] First, are subjects bound to obey the state if it commands that which is against the law of God? Second, is it lawful to resist a government which infringes the law of God and ruins the church? If so, who should exercise resistance, by what means, and how far is it lawful to extend resistance? Third, is it lawful to resist a government which oppresses and ruins a public state, and if so, how far should resistance be extended? Further, by whom, by what means, and by what right or law is it permitted? And fourth, are neighboring states permitted or compelled to aid the subjects of other states who are persecuted for true religion or oppressed by manifest tyranny? Briefly, the first question received a negative answer and the last three are answered in the affirmative.

The argument for the first consideration is based on the theory that "existing order in all states is based on two contracts."[62] The first issue is between God and his human subjects. The second is between the king (or governing ruler) and the people. In a situation where the commands of the two authorities are in conflict, the subject "is bound to obey the superior rather than the inferior lord."[63]

The answer to the second question "presents formally and completely the theory of contract as determining the reciprocal rights and duties of God, king, and people":[64]

> The first was that in which God, on the one hand, and the people and the king, on the other, engaged to maintain the ancient relation of the chosen people as the church of God; the second was that to which the king and the people were the parties, the former agreeing to rule justly and the latter to obey him. It is under the first of these two contracts that the right of the resistance to an impious prince is manifest.[65]

The latter contract or covenant "is specifically the political contract by which the people become a state; the king is bound by this agreement to rule well and justly, and the people to obey so long as he does":[66]

> [W]hereas the people's representatives swear a "conditional" obligation to the king, the king swears an "absolute" obligation to these representatives. . . . The outcome is said to be the creation of "a mutual obligation" between the king on the one hand and the magistrates on the other, an agreement

which "cannot be superseded by the other compact, or violated in the name of any other right." Mornay concludes the
section by insisting that the force of this contract is so great
"that a king who breaks it willfully may properly be called a
'tyrant,' while a people that breaks it may properly be called
'seditious.' "[67]

Du Plessis-Mornay's use of the word "tyrant" is significant.
To lawfully resist a tyrant, it was necessary to establish that the
monarch was guilty of tyranny. To Du Plessis-Mornay, "the tyrant is he who willfully disregards or violates the contract
through which alone monarchic dominion is legitimate."[68] Du
Plessis-Mornay and most other resistance writers were concerned with the consequences of what they wrote. In fact, the
Vindiciae denies the right of the individual to exercise tyranni-
cide. The ordinary citizen was bound, by the condition of his
citizenship, to submit to the governing body. However, it was
left to the "body of citizens" (or legislature or appointed representatives) to impose limits on the monarch or depose a tyrannical prince. Thus, the "body of citizens" serves as a check against
"mob rule." In short, the Calvinists drew a distinction between
lawless uprising and lawful resistance.

The third question renders an answer which "embodies a
complete and systematic demonstration of popular sovereignty
by divine right."[69] The king is the chosen instrument of God's
providential rule, and he reigns by the consent of the "elect."
"Monarchs were appointed to determine rights at home and to
lead armies abroad; but they always remain subject, in their
powers and actions, to the end for which they were created."[70]
When princes willfully neglected these responsibilities to the
detriment of the society, in breach of the social contract, the
Vindiciae advocated their deposition. The author of the Vindiciae, as did the American colonists, viewed the social contract—
a contract between the people and the state—as antistatist.

The fourth question is answered in the affirmative. "Since
the care of the church is recommended to the charge of Christian princes in general, they must not merely amplify it and
extend its boundaries where they can, but also, and in all places,
preserve it against attack."[71] The justification is, in other words,
to aid distressed and oppressed humanity. Translated in modern
terms, this would legitimize the United States, for example, mov-

ing against Communist bloc countries such as the Soviet Union which oppress people for exercising the rights to free speech, religion, and other fundamental guarantees.

A "CARRIER"

Through direct and indirect influences, both orthodox and liberal, "Locke became, in terms of his own medical profession, a 'carrier' of Calvinism from the Reformation to the revolutions of 1688 and 1776."[72] The political Calvinism assimilated and carried by Locke possessed the liberal, international character of the Calvinism founded or expanded by thousands of exiles for conscience' sake ("shrewd Genevan traders, prosperous Huguenot artisans and bankers, indomitable Dutch merchants, canny Scots, thrifty Scotch-Irish, and resourceful Puritans"), and the "Calvinists from all these lands who made up the majority of the seventeenth-century colonists in America."[73]

"The large and convincing mass of firsthand evidence," Foster writes, "proves that international [political] Calvinism filtered through Locke and the Revolution of 1688."[74] Obviously, these political and religious doctrines, among others, found their way to the American shores and came to fruition in 1776. Concerning the colonial Revolution, Americans did, indeed, make Lockean philosophy a "ground" of the Revolution. Moreover, these doctrines were not only heartedly received by the American clergy, but also were propounded on numerous occasions preceding the great conflict with Great Britain.

THE GOOD OF THE PEOPLE

*B*efore 1750 more than half the printed publications in the colonies were sermons.¹ Sermons by public request enriched the sessions of colonial legislatures. They solemnized days of fasting which were held at times of broad emergency. Moreover, the sermons lent counsel and advice, even as they offered up thanks for the occasions of joy and victory. The minister was a recognized source of opinion and guidance.

From a study of the colonial sermons, it becomes evident that the tenets of political Calvinism had been absorbed by the New England clergy. The New England clergy's total world view cannot be "viewed as representative of the religious rhetoric" of all thirteen colonies and their clergymen.² However, it can be asserted that because of the great impact of New England leadership—that lasted even up to the early 1900s—the New England clergy's viewpoints assumed a nationwide appeal.³

What had been preached in Europe as a political doctrine to oppose the tyranny of divine right would also serve as a basis for the American Revolution. Again we must recognize that the minister was influenced by many writers. Because of the theological makeup of the clergy, however, the doctrines of political Calvinism and related ideas were to serve as a primary source for the formation of the philosophy and ideology of the clergy and other colonial leaders.

This fact is extremely significant when one realizes the importance of the sermon in colonial life. For example, sermons preached at civil functions partook of the nature of judicial opinions:

The audience was accustomed to receive words from the minister's "desk" with much the same attitude which marked the reception of a judicial decision from the "bench." The preacher took pains, before his words were sent to the public in printed form, to justify by foot-notes such references as had a special bearing on the events of the day. One feature of many of the election sermons was a succession of particular applications to the various groups assembled; the governor and his councillors, the reverend clergy, and the people. To each was measured the meat of the discourse as it applied to the vocation concerned.[4]

Of particular importance for our discussion is the fact that the basic content in each of the grievances which ultimately found a place in the Declaration of Independence was a subject for pulpit analysis many years before the Declaration was drafted. The conclusion is, then, that many Reformation ideas (mixed with various other philosophies) as filtered through the New England clergy found a comfortable home in the Declaration of Independence. This fact is borne out by analysis of the content of the sermons of the colonial ministry.

LEGALLY MINDED MEN

The colonial clergy were legally minded men. Their theology and church polity had a legalistic cast which largely determined the character of their political thinking. For them, God's law did not concern religious and ecclesiastical matters alone but affected politics as well.

The New England clergy conceived the universe to be a great kingdom whose sovereign was God, whose relations with His Son, Jesus Christ, and with His creatures were determined by covenant or compact, "covenant-constitutions," which were always conditional and implied strict obligations on each side. Thus, we see the emergence of the compact theory of political Calvinism emerge in the colonial mind. As Alice M. Baldwin writes:

God had made a covenant of works with Adam and Eve, who willfully broke it. Then in His mercy He made a second covenant of grace "ordaining the Lord Jesus . . . according to a covenant made between them both, to be mediator between God and Man." This covenant made by Christ with His Father was entirely voluntary, a compact made between them in council. By it, salvation was promised to men in return for faith in the Christ. Christ, by His sacrifice, paid the penalty for a broken covenant which a just God, who ruled by law, could not but demand. In return, God gave into the hands of His Son, as His delegate, the government of the world. This conception of a covenant or compact as the foundation of divine and human relations is of basic importance in New England thought.[5]

The words of Reverend Samuel Belcher, who preached concerning "that blessed compact which passed between the Father and Son, when the Terms of Man's Redemption were agreed upon, in the Council of God,"[6] typified the thinking of the day.

The New England clergy commonly spoke of the divine law of God as a "divine constitution." This divine constitution was a fixed, fundamental law, sacred and inviolable. Throughout the seventeenth and eighteenth centuries it was a frequent theme of discussions. The clergy made it their goal to determine its nature and meaning and to make it clear to the people. They conceived of the fundamental law, a tenet of political Calvinism, as threefold, including the law of nature, the law of the Old Testament, and the law of Christ.

One of the most interesting features of the sermons and pamphlets during the early 1700s, as well as afterwards, is the treatment of the concept of the law of nature. By this is meant the general principles of justice and equity under which men are conceived to have lived before the founding of any society and civil state and which gave men their so-called "natural rights." This law of nature had been planted by God deep in the hearts of men. As Jonathan Mayhew (1720-1766) proclaimed, it is "written as with a pen of iron and the point of a diamond," before the fuller revelation of the written law came into existence, and was still to be found there.[7] Important here, however, is that there seems to be little evidence that the clergy, at least, thought of the so-called natural law as distinct from the law of God:

Thus in 1669 John Davenport in his Election Sermon said, "the Law of Nature is God's law." Again and again the clergy made this assertion and clearly regarded the laws of nature as sacredly and legally binding as any other part of the divine law. Samuel Hall in his Connecticut Election Sermon of 1746 put it thus: "I think there can be no doubt about this; but that in all cases where the matter under Determination appertains to natural Right, the Cause is God's Cause." John Barnard in his Massachusetts Election Sermon of 1734 phrased it somewhat differently but with equal assurance: "This Voice of Nature is the Voice of God. Thus 'tis that *vox populi est vox Dei.*"[8]

This law of nature was an unwritten law. The revelation in the Old and New Testaments helped to make clear the law of nature and to disclose its full extent. Therefore, we find in 1741 Reverend Solomon Williams in a sermon saying: "There never was, nor can be any Wisdom among men, but what is communicated from God; nor is there any Law of Nature, or Rule of Natural and Moral Wisdom, which we speak of, as implanted in the Mind of man, but what is found in the Bible, and cultivated and improved by that Revelation."[9]

From these premises it was taught that in the Old Testament God gave to man a "positive law," or written law. It was true that some of its statutes applied to Israel only, but there were also great moral principles which applied to all phases of man's activity, now as formerly, and were equally binding. Thus, even in that part of the Old Testament which no longer applied to Christians, and in the history of God's dealing with His chosen people, there were many examples for men today.

In the New Testament were the special laws made by Christ for His followers and His church. These did not in any way contradict the great laws of nature and the moral laws of the "Old Dispensation." In fact, some sermons go so far as to speak of Christ as having a "natural right" to the government of men, as a result of His covenant or contract with God.[10]

It was commonly taught by the clergy that this law of God, natural and written, was not only moral but also rational. "God expected obedience not so much because of His authority as because of its reasonableness and the benefits to be derived therefrom. The good of His people and the rights of men were the end of His government and His law was framed with that in view."[11]

In 1755, Reverend Jonathan Mayhew declared: "No one but God has an absolute, unlimited authority over us."[12] However, God did not act in an arbitrary and unjust fashion. He could not. The very nature of God forbade it, because he was a perfect God. Thus, His every act must be perfectly just. As such, the laws of nature and the revealed law, being God's law, were expressions of this perfection. God, therefore, by His very nature, was bound by them.

Even those clergy who did not agree fully with the Calvinists did not deny the fact of God's absolute sovereignty. It was taught that as God is a reasonable and lawful God, so must be the rulers of the earth. Thus, we find Mayhew in 1750 arguing: "God Himself does not govern in an absolute arbitrary and despotic manner. The Power of this almighty King is limited by law—by the external laws of truth, wisdom, and equity, and the everlasting tables of right reason."[13] Thus, clergy, by and large, believed in a divine law, a fundamental constitution, which was binding upon God and man. From this, long before 1776, the New England clergy included the so-called laws of nature as well as Christ's "law of liberty" as part of their politico-religious doctrines.

These ministerial teachings are fundamental in any understanding of American constitutional thought. The clergy taught that "God's government is founded on and limited by law and therefore all human governments must be so founded and limited, if patterned after His. A government, therefore, which exercises its authority unconstitutionally acts illegally. Here is one great source of the American doctrine of government by law."[14]

CONCEPTS OF GOVERNMENT

Long before 1776 the New England clergy had developed and expounded an elaborate theory of government. As they founded their theology and church polity upon the law of God as revealed in the natural law and the written word, so from the law of God they developed their political theories. They read histories, ancient and modern, pored over commentaries, and studied the works of philosophers when they could get them. However, "even the most learned turn to the infallible Scripture to learn what God intended government should be."[15]

Civil government, so the clergy taught, was of divine origin. Sometimes they founded their arguments on reason or the "light" and law of nature, sometimes on the Bible, sometimes on both, but it amounted to the same thing in the end. Government was ordained of God, and its purpose, like the government of Christ and of God Himself, was the good of the people. As a minister articulated in 1725: "And a good Ruler knows these Maxims are not only founded in Nature, but expressly asserted in God's Word. . . . All shall be Sacrificed to subserve the Publick."[16] And as Mayhew argued in 1754: "The end of government, then, as it is a divine ordinance, must be human felicity... must be the common good of all, and of every individual, so far as consistent therewith."[17]

The analogy between theology and political theory is very close and very significant. Even the most conservative of the clergy admitted it. The more liberal of the clergy emphasized it. A government which did not have the good of the people at heart did not have the sanction of God. There could be no other end, whether government were considered as a divine ordinance, instituted indirectly by God, or as more immediately the ordinance of man, founded in common consent and for the good of the people. Another tenet of political Calvinism emerges. Neither God nor man had any other purpose in founding government. Alice Baldwin writes:

> This was the starting place for the necessity of law and order, for the limitation upon rulers, and for the inviolability of the rights and liberties of people. From it sprang the argument, identical with that of Locke, that governments are limited by the purpose for which they were founded . . . the good of the people. The good of the people might be interpreted variously, but whatever else it meant it assured the protection of their natural rights. Without government there would be no security for those rights which God intended man to enjoy, no assurance of life, good order, liberty, and prosperity.[18]

It was commonly taught by the clergy that, except in the case of Israel, God did not specify the particular type of government to be established. Men, therefore, might choose, provided always that the type chosen answered the proper end of government and was not inconsistent with the divine laws.

The clergy asserted that civil government, though ordained

by God, did not come immediately from the Creator, but *mediately* through the people. Moreover, whatever form government might take, the clergy almost unanimously agreed that if it were a just government it had been founded on "compact":

> This compact relationship was a matter of vital importance to the New England minister. His theology depended upon it, it was the foundation of his church government, he believed it to be at the root of all God's dealings with men. When he searched the Bible he found, so he believed, that even the Jewish government, which was peculiarly God's own, rested on compact. When he questioned Reason and Nature, which to him were the voice of God, again he found the compact or covenant. When he read the wise men of the past and of his own day, once more he found it. When he looked at his own environment he found it there. The charters were considered compacts, and when men set up new towns they drew up a town covenant. It became in practical experience the only way to form a corporate body.[19]

Again political Calvinism surfaces in the form of the compact theory of government. Thus, the compact seems to have been accepted without question by the ministers of both the seventeenth and eighteenth centuries. As such, both the "social" or governmental as well as church covenants were used to explain and defend the rights of the people in church and state, and not only of the people but of rulers also.

These principles or concepts of government were articulated by a varied number of clergy. For example, Roger Williams proclaimed: "The sovereign, original, and foundation of civil power lies in the people; and it is evident that such governments are by them erected and established, have no more power, nor for no longer time, than the civil power or people consenting and agreeing shall betrust them with. This is clear, not only in reason, but in the experience of all commonweals, where the people are not deprived of their natural freedom by the power of tyrants."[20]

There seems to have been a basic agreement that government is established by the people and rests upon their consent; that magistrates are chosen by the people and are strictly limited both in power and in exercise of it. Consistent with the theory of the compact-consent of the people is the concept that rulers are removable if they violate the conditions of authority entrusted to them by the people and God.

Probably the most complete account of the process by which compacts were made was that of John Wise, a minister who had been in prison for refusing to pay taxes that had been levied against him. He expressed his views in a treatise, famous in his day, that he published in 1717 entitled *A Vindication of the Government of New England Churches*. This treatise is a striking argument for democracy in church and state and, because of its popularity, had a remarkable effect.

Wise considered man first in his natural state, enjoying the liberty which belonged to him, a liberty which made him subject to no other human being. In consequence, he argued, all men in this state of nature were equal in authority and each had a right to judge for himself what was most conducive to his happiness and welfare. This liberty and equality of men, so Wise believed, could not be lessened until, in order to form a civil state, they gave up certain rights (at the same time preserving and cherishing as much as was consistent with the public good). The people were, therefore, the origin of *all* power. However, when the people combined in society, they delegated a part of their power and authority to others; that is, the government. Wise concluded that a democracy was the type of government which the "light of nature" often directed men toward. Wise proclaimed: "A democracy, This is a form of government, which the light of nature does highly value, and often directs to, as most agreeable to the just and natural prerogative of human beings."[21]

It may appear in the philosophy of Wise and other American clergy that they were drawing their arguments strictly from natural law theory rather than biblical theology. As we have seen, the leaders of the eighteenth century, as those of the seventeenth century, believed reason and nature to be the voice of God. Also, the laws of nature were truly those of God as made more clear through the revelation of the Bible. For example, Reverend Solomon Williams in a sermon delivered in 1741 in Connecticut said: "There never was nor can be any wisdom among men, but what is communicated from God; nor is there any Law of Nature, or Rule of Natural and Moral wisdom, which we speak of, as implanted in the Mind of man, but what is found in the Bible, and cultivated and improved by that Revelation. . . . Here Rulers are taught to seek the virtue and happiness of their People, as the end of Government."[22]

It is evident that the majority of the clergy believed, as did Reverend Elisha Williams, that all governments which did not originate from the people and in which they did not make their own laws were not, properly speaking, governments at all, but tyrannies and "absolutely against the Law of God and Nature."[23] Thus, there was no medium between common consent and lawless force and violence.

RULERS

Reverend Samuel Stoddard in a sermon in 1703 made the assertion: "The abuses that are offered unto a People by their Rulers, and the abuses that are offered unto the Rulers by the People are deeply resented by God."[24] Over half a century later Benjamin Stevens, in a similar sermon, declared: "The Majesty of laws must be revered, where the liberties of a people are secured."[25] Thus, the New England ministers commonly applied the concept of compact obligations, natural law, and God-given rights to their conception of the relative power and duties of rulers and the people. All this had already been set forth years before the likes of Thomas Jefferson and others began espousing similar ideas.

By 1715, a period of rapid growth in the New England colonies had set in:

> Men began to move into the western part of Massachusetts and the less settled regions of Connecticut and up along the rivers into Vermont and New Hampshire. They were eager for land, even to the extent of buying it when they had no intention of settling. New towns were founded, old ones were divided. There were quarrels between absentee proprietors and settlers, quarrels over land titles, quarrels over church affairs and over many other matters. There were wars, bitter party strife, struggles between the lower and upper houses of the legislature, disputes with the governors, depreciation of the currency, speculation, greater differentiation in wealth, hard times for the poor.[26]

A consequence of this rapid growth was a widespread discontent among the people. Men were inclined to ignore distinctions of rank and to criticize the government, to talk vaguely of equality and liberty, of oppression and the burdens of heavy taxes.

Some of the clergy blamed the people and emphasized the

need of submission to government and to authority. Others did not hesitate to lay a large share of the trouble at the doors of the governing authorities and to enlarge upon the duties of rulers to the people. The Bible, so these argued, was far more concerned with the good of subjects than with the splendor of rulers. Thus, the main topic of political sermons and many of those more purely religious was what constituted lawful authority. Again, the clergy searched the Bible and the law of God as well as the writings of philosophers, ancient and modern.

The ministers of New England believed that "rulers," among whom they included the king, parliament, colonial governors and assemblies, and all authorities, were God's delegates and derived their power from the Creator. However, the power to rulers from God was not derived directly from God. It was folly to think such things and to base thereon any claim to absolute authority or divine right. Rather, the power came, as did civil government itself, mediately from God but directly from the people.

Therefore, in 1750 Jonathan Mayhew could argue: "These notions are not drawn from the holy scriptures, but from a far less sure and sacred foundation. They are only the devices of lawned parasites, or other graceless politicians, to serve the purposes of ambition and tyranny."[27] John Barnard, in his sermon of 1734, preached: "So that after all is said, the Right to rule takes its Rise from the Consent, and Agreement, that is the Choice and Election, of the Community, State, or Kingdom . . . and He, and He only, has the Right to rule, to whom the Government commits the Power, and Authority."[28]

It was not left to rulers to be oppressive and arbitrary, not even if their power came by conquest. God, from whom their power ultimately was derived, had limited that power. The governing authorities had received their power as delegated from God, but they must conform to God's pattern and must labor to imitate God's government. In a 1744 sermon, James Allen asserted that the "great end of government is the good of the subject: This is the very design of Christ Himself in his rule over us. . . . Now in this the God of heaven is a pattern to our earthly Gods."[29]

Again, the analogy between theology and political philosophy emerges. God and Christ govern men for their good, and so must human rulers. As Joseph Belcher preached in 1701, the

Bible illustrated very clearly how Joshua, Moses, David, and Solomon had only the good of the people at heart.[30] For that and that only does government exist.

The theory enunciated by many clergy was that God and Christ governed always by fixed rules, by divine constitution, and therefore so must human rulers. Baldwin notes:

> The fundamental constitution of states may differ; men's rights under them may be greater or less, but certain great rights are given by Nature and Nature's God to the people. These are a part of every constitution and no ruler is permitted by God to violate them. Rulers cannot change the constitution; that can be done only by the people. But the constitution and the laws must be consonant with the divine law. . . . In the Bible are found all maxims and rules of government: there the natural laws are made clearer, there the ruler learns his due authority and its limitations, there the people learn how far they must submit. Rulers must also thoroughly understand the constitution and the civil law, that they may learn their obligation and the people's rights. Even when God dealt with the Jews who were under His immediate government, He had their rulers write down the constitution in a book and read it constantly.[31]

Not only are the rulers strictly limited by law, but the people are as well, argued the clergy. To submit to lawful authority is required of them by God. This did not mean a lessening but rather a preservation of their liberty, for law is the basis for liberty. Without law and obedience to law, there would be no liberties. Lawlessness on the part of the people is quite as likely to destroy it as tyranny and oppression on the part of rulers. Neither tyranny nor anarchy is pleasing to God, the clergy argued.

One of the most striking features of the political philosophy of the ministers is the emphasis upon the fundamental law and its binding quality. Gershom Bulkeley in 1692 wrote that no human law can be contrary to the law of nature and right reason for an unreasonable law is a law against law, and unlawful authority is no authority.[32]

In 1713 John Bulkley of Connecticut preached a sermon wherein he argued that religion inculcates good principles, establishes maxims of government, forces both ruled and ruler to a faithful performance of duty. He argued against arbitrary rulers, asserting that no power can be vested in men which is not proportioned to the public good. Bulkley argued: "No Law of the Civil Magistrate can bind in Opposition to the Divine."[33] He then states that it is "a Sin . . . to invade these Rights of a People."[34]

That rulers must preserve the life, liberty, and property of the people inviolate or else act in opposition to God's law is an ideal repeated constantly in sermons and pamphlets written by the clergy in the early 1700s:

> From the middle of the seventeenth century this is a common phrase, especially liberty and property. The significance of this is great and cannot be overemphasized. No one can fully understand the American Revolution and the American constitutional system without a realization of the long history and religious associations which lie back of these words; without realizing that for a hundred years before the Revolution men were taught that these rights were protected by divine, inviolable law.[35]

As such, John Hancock in 1722, the predecessor of Jonas Clark of Revolutionary fame and the grandfather of the more famous John Hancock, in a sermon could assert: "As Oppression makes a wise man mad, so it makes a righteous God angry."[36]

In 1738 Jared Eliot, a pastor and a friend and correspondent of Benjamin Franklin, wrote that if any laws should be made by a government which are inconsistent with the laws of God or which sapped the foundations of the commonwealth, men must exercise their right of discretion and must obey God rather than men, as did the Apostles.[37]

Likewise, Jonathan Mayhew in 1754 preached a sermon in which he argued against any concept of unlimited submission to government. He declared that "[n]either God nor nature has given any man a right of dominion over any society independently of that society's approbation and consent to be governed by him."[38] Mayhew then goes on to state, "Disobedience is not only lawful but glorious" in response to those that "enjoin things that are inconsistent with the demands of God."[39]

IMBEDDING

From the sermons of the clergy, the continuity and strength of political principles, and their intimate connection to the Bible and Reformation thought, the truths of liberty were, by continuous repetition over a period of years, deeply imbedded in the colonial mind. The concept of the rights of men and their assertion against statist interference were articulated long before 1776. The next step, therefore, was the right to resist government. That too was consonant with the tenor of the day.

SEVEN

THE REVOLT OF THE BLACK REGIMENT

*I*n the 1740s the Great Awakening swept through colonial America. It deeply affected men's emotions and thinking.[1]

The Great Awakening intensified the belief in fundamental law. It, along with the preaching that preceded it, led to the belief that any systematic violation of the fundamental rights of men by governing authorities was tyranny. Furthermore, revolt against such tyranny was not only legal but a *religious duty.*

Soon the talk concerning "unalienable" rights grew more common. References to John Locke and other so-called radical theorists began to proliferate.

THE AWAKENING

There had been signs of a stirring of the spirit here and there in New England, notably under the preaching of Jonathan Edwards (1703-1758). However, it was not until the arrival of George Whitefield (1714-1770) in New England in 1740 that a revival swept through the country.

Certain of Whitefield's teachings are of special significance. A Calvinist himself, this Englishman appears to have been at least indirectly influenced by some of the presuppositions of political Calvinism that were prevalent to the European community of his day.

Whitefield believed that there were certain fundamental divine laws which a Christian subject must first obey. However, he argued that Christians had the right to question and, if necessary, to break rules and laws that were contrary to these principles.

Second, Whitefield taught that all men, rich and poor, wise and ignorant, shared in the gospel of Christ. Thus, all men were equal in the fellowship of Christ. Thus, the common man crowded to hear him. Whitefield went so far as to say that a learned ministry was unnecessary. This eventually led to many gathering about simple men who felt themselves inspired of God to preach. This obvious doctrine of equal rights would soon have strong political implications.

Third, Whitefield had a tolerance, unusual in his day, of all kinds of church government and creeds. This was a tolerance far too broad to admit of any alliance between church and state. In Philadelphia, he once exclaimed:

> "Father Abraham, who have you in heaven? Any Episcopalians?" "No." "Any Presbyterians?" "No." "Any Baptists?" "No." "Any Methodists, Seceders, or Independents?" "No, No!" "Why, who have you there?" "We don't know those names here. All who are here are Christians." Oh, is that the case? Then, God help me! And God help us all to forget party names and to become Christians in deed and truth.[2]

These beliefs were proclaimed in sermons that were heard by thousands of people as Whitefield preached from the pulpit and from courthouse steps. They were read by thousands more as edition after edition was published and scattered throughout the country.

During his first visit to America, the ministers welcomed him. Churches and colleges were freely open to his preaching. When the implications of his preaching became clear, however, controversy followed.

Whitefield could not travel through the colonies without arousing angry opposition and bitter strife, and more so his followers, who shared his earnestness but lacked his tolerant spirit. In his published journal were unflattering accounts of the American ministry and the colleges. He called many of the former "unconverted" and the latter homes of darkness rather than light.[3]

The Awakening, through the preaching of Whitefield and others, fomented a spirit of questioning and discussions in the colonies as well as a testing of authorities by "new" standards. Students began to criticize their tutors, congregations their ministers; laymen, some of whom were of poor class, took it upon themselves to preach and exhort. Soon men were divided into

"Old Lights," those who opposed the movement, and "New Lights," of whom the most extreme were known as "Separates" or "Strict Congregationalists."

Soon some of the leading ministers and governing authorities of the colleges tried to suppress the movement. This was to no avail. Soon the Great Awakening had spread over the entire country.

The revival brought on by the Great Awakening was America's first truly national event. "The revival in short began to provide a set of common experiences for the colonies which marked them off as, together, a unified region distinct from Europe."[4]

In addition, as Americans began to regard themselves more distinctly in colony-wide terms, "they naturally became more suspicious of churches which retained secure ties with Europe":

> The most important of these was the Church of England, which was already suspect by some for its close ties with crown officials. After the Awakening, it became a focus of even more suspicion because of its relative indifference to the spread of revival. Such religious feelings had definite political ramifications when tempers between the colonies and the British government began to flare. Suspicion of the Church of England was one more reason for distrusting the British in general.[5]

Curious was the attempt of Parliament to force the establishment of the Church of England on the colonies. Because of the widespread opposition by the colonial clergy, this action, as much as any other cause, was important for a rethinking of the colonies' relationship to Great Britain.[6] As John Adams recognized: "The objection was not merely to the office of a bishop, though even that was dreaded, but to the authority of parliament, on which it was founded."[7]

The Great Awakening also made it respectful to use terms like "liberty," "virtue," and "tyranny" in public discussion. Moreover, other terms such as "equality" and "revolution" and "resistance" became more prevalent in colonial language.

The most important factor of the revival on the Revolutionary period may have been the new model of leadership which it created. The revival was nurtured by traveling evangelists. They called for direct and responsible response from the people and encouraged lay people to perform Christian services for themselves that were usually the traditional preserve of the clergy.

Moreover, Whitefield did not read his sermons as so many ministers did in the early eighteenth century. Rather, he used spontaneous, extemporaneous forms of address:

> His speaking style drove home the implicit point that it was not formal education or a prestigious place in the community that mattered ultimately. It was rather the choice of the individual, the common person, for or against God. Whitefield seems to have had almost no thought for politics. But his form of public speaking, and the implicit message of his ministry concerning leadership, constituted a powerful stimulus to a more democratic life. It was not Whitefield alone, of course, who was responsible. But he was the most visible symbol of a vital change in ideas about social hierarchy.[8]

His ministry represented the sharpest demonstration of a new confidence "in the religious powers of the people."[9] Whitefield was a Calvinist who did not believe in natural human capacity to choose God. But he did believe that God's grace made it possible for even the humblest individual to take a place alongside the greatest of the saints. "This spirit—a frank expression of popular democracy and the sharpest attack yet on inherited privilege in colonial America—probably had much to do with the rise of a similar spirit in politics later on."[10]

Numerous historians have recognized that the Great Awakening was a tremendous spur to the coming of American democracy. The Great Awakening, therefore, had a number of democratizing effects.

First, the Awakening brought on the revival of piety which accelerated the trend toward multiplication of religions. All those liberating social forces which derived from the splintering of the sects were given added emphasis by the schisms created in Congregationalism and Presbyterianism, by the founding of new and short-lived churches on the frontier, and by the breaking of ground for the coming of Methodism.[11]

Second, the increase in the number of dissenting churches and the upsurge of fervor in men and women of all denominations gave new strength to the campaign for separation of church and state. "Certainly disestablishment and religious liberty would not have come so swiftly in Virginia had not the Great Awakening helped create a social situation in which any other course would have been impractical and disruptive."[12]

Third, equality rather than liberty or fraternity was the chief beneficiary of the Great Awakening.

> The revival spirit placed emphasis on the importance of the regenerated individual, without regard to his social standing, national background, calling, or religion. The rise of personalized religion among the poor folk of the colonies gave a lift to those doctrines of individual worth and social equality which were to lead the new nation to Jacksonian democracy. By insisting that heaven, the greatest prize of all, was open to all men on equal terms, the preachers of the Awakening aroused leveling sentiments among tens of thousands of common men.[13]

Fourth, a natural result of these new feelings of individualism and equality was the further democratizing of organization and methods in the churches. More democracy in the church led in turn to more democracy in the community, and so the great historical interaction of religion and politics continued to work to liberate the people.

Fifth, if the Great Awakening led many people to distrust learning and intelligence and to insist that their ministers be no better than they, it led other men, "especially Presbyterians," to a more lively concern for education—an example of the mixed character of such broadly popular movements.

> William Tennent's "Log College" at Neshaminy, Pennsylvania, was the most important boost to education at the time of the Great Awakening; Princeton, Brown, Rutgers, Dartmouth, Washington and Lee, and Hampden-Sydney are modern reminders of the thorough shaking-up visited upon colonial society by the Great Awakening.[14]

Sixth, still another product of eighteenth-century revivalism was an increase in social consciousness and humanitarianism. Some historians trace the beginnings of the antislavery movement in America to the egalitarian preachings of men like Samuel Hopkins, "and certainly several left-wing sects emerged from this period with new and radical attitudes on Negro slavery. The Great Awakening also revived interest in Indian missions, and everywhere there was renewed concern for abnormal and unfortunate members of society."[15]

Finally, the revival aroused latent feelings of class antagonism. It appealed primarily to the poor and "despised." It revolted the well-born, well-educated, and well-to-do. "As a result, it spread like wildfire among Baptists, stirred up bitter opposition against Anglicans, and split the Presbyterian, Congregational, and Reformed churches into conservative and radical factions that conformed amazingly to class lines."[16]

The challenge of religious radicalism to the formalistic religion of the ruling class carried with it new doubts about the claims of this class to social and political superiority. In most parts of the country, the old habits of deference were weakened severely by the Great Awakening. As a result of the influences of the Great Awakening, by 1765 religion in the colonies had taken on a new and unmistakable look and would henceforth be recognized as "characteristically American." Denominations began to blend and there appeared a diversity of doctrine and organization, with no one church claiming anything like a clear majority. "The result of their blending in the colonial environment was a pattern of faith more individualistic and liberating than that of any other Christian land."[17]

THE CLERGY SPEAKS OUT

In 1744 a pamphlet published by Elisha Williams, a follower of George Whitefield, gave a full discussion of equality and liberty. Williams defines natural liberty as freedom from any superior earthly power and subjection only to the law of nature, which he declares to be the law of God. Williams also argues for a natural right to property. He writes:

> As Reason tells us, all are born thus naturally equal, i.e. with an equal Right to their Persons; so also with an equal Right to their Preservation; and therefore to such Things as Nature affords for their Subsistence. . . . Thus every Man having a natural Right to . . . his own Person and his Actions and Labour, which we call Property; it certainly follows, that no

Man can have a Right to the Person or Property of another:
And if every Man has a Right to his Person and Property; he
has also a Right to defend them, and a Right to all the
necessary Means of Defence, and so has a Right of punishing
all Insults upon his Person and Property.[18]

Williams essentially espouses a Lockean philosophy, as well
as principles enunciated during the Great Awakening. This is
reflected in his statement that the powers of government are
limited: "[T]heir power is a limited one: and therefore the Obedience due is a limited Obedience."[19]

As to what people must do to free themselves from tyranny,
Williams again refers to Locke. Thus, here is a minister of 1744
using the very arguments of the 1770s, declaring that subjects
and rulers are bound by a constitution and that a law violating
natural and constitutional rights is no law and requires no obedience:

Here is clear evidence of the transmission through the clergy
of the theories of Locke. The importance of this and like
pamphlets is this: they show how the thinking and the theory that came out in the Revolutionary period were uttered
not alone in theoretical sermons but in practical disputes and
controversies over church and individual rights long before
the trouble with England arose.[20]

There are also a number of other sermons and pamphlets that
address the theories of Locke and political Calvinism before the
1770s and before the conflict with Great Britain began to heat
up.

Many sermons also advanced the proposition that laws in
contradiction to natural rights were null and void. When Jonathan Mayhew, in 1673, said that true religion comprised the love
of liberty and of one's country and the hatred of all tyranny and
oppression, he was expressing the common convictions of the
New England ministry that the civil liberty which they cherished
so dearly received its chief sanction from their religious faith.[21]

As the conflict with Great Britain became more imminent,
the clergy became stronger in their outspokenness against oppressive government. It is sometimes through the eyes of an
enemy that a man's or a group's power can best be seen. Peter

Oliver, the last chief justice under the colonial regime in Massachusetts, held the dissenting ministers in detestation as the henchmen of patriot James Otis (1725-1783). Otis, says Oliver, saw from the beginning the necessity of securing "the black Regiment" if he were to rouse the people.[22] The clergy, or "black Regiment" as they were called because of the color of their clerical robes, were recognized by the British as the key to fanning the flames of resistance among the people.

In 1769 Jason Haven of Boston, in a sermon which was widely read and which met with special notice of England, spoke of the fall of Charles I and of the right of Massachusetts to elect its council, a right which he hoped might continue to the end of time. He quoted Locke on the right of resistance to every encroachment upon natural and constitutional rights, and asserted the right of people to call those in authority to account and take away their power when abused.[23]

Another method by which the ministers promoted opposition to England in these years as well as later was through their association with young men in the colleges. As teachers, they inculcated principles of government and permitted debates on questions which caused some disturbance. For example, in the new Brown University the students debated in 1769 whether it was good policy for the Americans under present conditions to establish an independent state.[24] Baldwin writes:

> Andrew Eliot, a somewhat conservative man though constantly friendly to the American cause, said in 1769 that the Harvard students had imbibed the spirit of the times and that their declamations and debates were full of the spirit of liberty. This, he said, had been encouraged, even if sometimes it got out of bounds, because their tutors were afraid to check too decidedly a spirit which might thereafter fill the country with patriots.[25]

The Boston Massacre of March 1770 greatly excited the populace. Again, the clergy was partly responsible. For example, the Sunday after the Massacre, John Lathrop of the Old North Church preached a sermon on the text, "The voice of thy brother's blood cryeth under me from the ground."[26]

Chief Justice Oliver was especially bitter against the clergy during these days. Before the trials of the men involved in the

Boston Massacre he said that the "Pulpits rang their Chimes upon blood Guiltiness, in Order to incite the People" and, after the trials were over, again the pulpits "rang their Peals of Malice against the Courts of Justice."[27] Moreover, another observer noted that the people were led by such sermons to feel that they might as lawfully resist the king's truths as those of a foreign enemy.[28]

Reverend Isaac Skillman published a pamphlet in which he asserted the right of the Americans—if they united, as he thought there was a good prospect of their doing—to resist any military force, a right which they had "by the law of God, of nature and of nations."[29] Skillman went on to argue: "Shall a man be deem'd a rebel that supports his own rights? it is the first law of nature, and he must be a rebel to God, to the laws of nature, and his own conscience, who will not do it."[30]

In May of 1774, a gentlemen of New York wrote to his friend in London excoriating the clergy of New England for their "most wicked, malicious and inflammatory harangues . . . spiriting their godly hearers to the most violent opposition to Government; persuading them that the intention of the Government was to rule them with a rod of iron, and to make them all slaves; and assuring them that if they would rise as one man to oppose these arbitrary schemes, God would assist them."[31]

As the British Parliament exercised its alleged authority to control the colonies by passing various laws and acts, the clergy preached resistance. Simultaneously, they increased in power.

By 1774, the Boston ministers were even refusing to read any proclamations of the British-appointed governor and council. When General Gage refused to appoint a day of fasting and prayer because "the request was only to give an opportunity for sedition to flow from the pulpit," the response was quick.[32] Political sermons, some of them violent in tone, were preached from Boston. The Provincial Congress in Massachusetts requested the clergy to advise strict obedience to the Continental Congress and to "make the question of the rights of the colonies and the oppressive conduct of the mother country a topic of the pulpit on weekdays."[33] Thus, the Continental Congress recognized the value of these politico-religious sermons. Many of these same sermons were published as patriotic pamphlets.[34]

It is important to note here that because of the lack of anything comparable to modern media, essentially the only place the people received news and received the doctrine of resistance was from the pulpit. As one observer noted: "During the entire Revolutionary period, the latter [clergy] were leaders and the most potent factors in resistance to British oppression. . . . In the absence of a numerous newspaper press, the political education of the people then as now in sparsely settled regions was conducted largely from the pulpit—or the stump."[35]

Resistance became something that was preached and something that was to be desired "at all costs." The sermons took on a radical tone. For example, soon after a town was burned in August of 1775, a recruiting officer who was vainly trying to raise men in Harpswell, Maine, asked Reverend Samuel Eaton, a patriotic minister of the town, to speak on Sunday morning to his people. Unwilling to do this at the Communion service, he promised to address them in the evening. Thus, after sundown, out of doors before the meetinghouse steps, he preached on the text, "Cursed be he that keepeth back his sword from blood."[36] Before the night was over, forty men had volunteered to serve in the American cause.

In all these sermons and like sermons and addresses, the chief aim seems to have been to state clearly and repeatedly the arguments by which men could be certain that they had inalienable rights. Also, these sermons were designed to set forth in detail the requirements of a legally constituted government and to show that the English and colonial governments, if unabused, were such. They also sought to enumerate and enlarge upon the acts by which king and Parliament had abused their power and to establish beyond a doubt a legal right and moral necessity of resistance.

It must be understood that the clergy's idea of resistance to unconstitutional acts did not mean refusal to obey constitutional authority. Far from it. "Though recognizing the provocation to violence and though sometimes encouraging abuse of the Tories, there was many a minister who drew careful distinction between liberty and license. It was the liberty which was to their minds inextricably associated with constitutional, ordered government for which they were fighting."[37]

Resistance thus became a sacred duty to a people who still were, on the whole, a religious people. Moreover, with the preaching of this resistance it is evident that the New England clergy, especially the Congregationalists, were preaching independence and preparing for independence long before 1776.

THE CLERGY AND THE DECLARATION

In June of 1776 the Continental Congress appointed a committee of five to draft a Declaration of Independence. Thomas Jefferson, the first member chosen for the committee, served as chairman and wrote the first draft of the Declaration. Jefferson and others are often given monumental importance in forming the political mindset of their day. Unfortunately, however, the great influence of the clergy is, again, often omitted by historians. But the impact of clergy may be even greater than previously suspected.[38] This is reflected in the writings of a number of ministers. One such clergyman who seems to have assisted in forming the basic philosophical foundations that later found their way into the Declaration of Independence is Reverend Samuel West (1730-1807).

On May 29, 1776, Samuel West addressed the Council House of Representatives in Boston. This address occurred some weeks before Jefferson began drafting the Declaration of Independence. West proclaimed:

> The only difficulty remaining is to determine when a people may claim a right of *forming themselves into a body politick,* and may *assume the powers of legislation.* In order to determine this point, we are to remember, that *all men being by nature equal,* all members of a community have a *natural right* to assemble themselves together, and to act and vote for such regulations, as they judge are necessary for the good of the whole. But when a community is become very numerous, it is very difficult, and in many cases impossible for all to meet together to regulate the affairs of the state: Hence comes the necessity of appointing delegates to represent the people in a general assembly. And this ought to be look'd upon as a sacred and *unalienable right,* of which a people cannot justly divest themselves, and which no human authority can in equity ever take from them . . . that no one be obliged to submit to any laws except such as are made either by himself, or by his representative.
>
> If representation and legislation are inseparably connected, it follows, that when great numbers have emigrated into a foreign land, and are so far removed from the parent state, that they neither are or can be properly represented by the government from which they have emigrated, that then *nature* itself points out the necessity of their *assuming to them-*

selves the powers of legislation, and they have a right *to consider themselves as a separate state* from the other, and as such to *form themselves into a body politick.*

When a people find themselves cruelly oppressed by the parent state, they have an *undoubted right to throw off the yoke,* and to assert their liberty, if they find good reason to judge that they have sufficient power and strength to maintain their ground in defending their just rights against their oppressors: For in this case by the law of self preservation, which is the first *law of nature,* they have not only an *undoubted right,* but it is their *indispensable duty,* if they cannot be redressed any other way, to renounce all submission to the government that has oppressed them, and *set up an independent state* of their own; even tho' they may be vastly inferior in number to the state that has oppress'd them. When either of the afore-said cases takes place, and more especially when both concur, no rational man (I imagine,) can have any doubt in his own mind, whether such a people have *a right to form themselves into a body politick,* and assume to themselves all the powers of a free state.[39]

The words of Samuel West bear a striking resemblance to the words and phraseology found in the Declaration of Independence. Their similarity becomes clear when the parallel passages from the two documents are arranged in columns:

Declaration	*West*
Laws of Nature	law of nature
all men are created equal	all men being by nature equal
unalienable rights	unalienable right
it is their right	undoubted right
it is their duty	indispensable duty
throw off such a government	throw off the yoke
institute new government	forming themselves into a body politick
separate and equal station	to consider themselves a separate state
assume among the powers	assuming to themselves the powers of legislation

Obviously the Declaration of Independence reflects a broad range of colonial clerical preaching more than it does any single sermon. Also, the clergy were sounding boards for the writings of varied political pamphleteers, as they were often the companions of many of the leaders. They were contributors to the thought of men who ran the legislatures and journeyed to the Continental Congress. John Adams, in his diary, even recalls phrases which were favorites with one preacher he had heard.[40] Adams, as did others, cherished the studied expressions on matters of deep public concern which the clergy preached and often published.

In short, colonial sermons formed a solid base of integrated thought. Founded upon the Bible, they made up a large part of the contribution of the philosophy of freedom which began to win a worldwide empire in the minds of men through the conflict which arose with Great Britain. And it would eventually assume a common fabric of rights, resistance, and futuristic optimism within the American psyche.

RIGHTS AND RESISTANCE

"**N**ever was there a People," wrote a colonist in 1768, "whom it more immediately concerned to search into the Nature and Extent of their Rights and Privileges than it does the People of America at this Day."[1] They also searched for basic principles that would justify these rights and give them substance.

The principles in which the American colonists placed their special trust were those taught by the clergy, the oldest of libertarian philosophy, and the school of natural law. The practical purpose of the colonists was to limit the power of Parliament, and like all men with the slightest feeling for abstract justice, they sought limits more universal than those staked out in laws, charters, and constitutions. The great philosophy that preached the reality and moral restraints on power had always been a part of their Anglo-Christian heritage.[2] The eloquence of the patriot leaders, which in large part was composed of the clergy, changed this philosophy from "a commonplace of morality" to "a mass of dynamite."[3] With this dynamite they proceeded to blow up an empire.

After organizing their Anglo-Christian heritage into a political philosophy, these men addressed the state of nature, the law of nature, the nature of man, the natural rights of man, civil rights, and the right of resistance. These principles of rights and resistance became part and parcel of the American dream.

NEWTON AND NATURE
As we have seen, the concept of a state of nature and the law or laws of nature was an important conceptual framework in the

molding of the revolutionary mind. Nature nearly assumed a deified character. In this deification of nature, a decisive influence must be ascribed to Isaac Newton (1642-1727), whose great work, the *Principia*, was first published in 1686. This book had a tremendous impact on the thinkers of the seventeenth and eighteenth centuries, including John Locke and the leading colonial thinkers as well as the clergy.

Newton's demonstration that the force (gravity) which brings the apple to the ground is the same force that holds the planets in their orbits stirred his contemporaries with the picture of a universe which is pervaded with the same reason which shines in man and is accessible in all its parts to exploration by man. Between a universe "lapt in law" and the human mind all barriers were cast down. Inscrutable deity, then, became scrutable nature. English deism, it has been wittily remarked, "deified Nature and denatured God."[4]

However, one section of nature is human nature and its institutions. "With Newton's achievement at their back men turned confidently to the formulation of the inherently just and reasonable rules of social and political relationship. Entire systems were elaborated which purported to deduce with Euclidean precision the whole duty of man, both moral and legal, from a few agreed premises."[5]

Newton was a deeply religious man. Throughout his lifetime he tried to be loyal to what he believed concerning Christian principles. It has been said that many seventeenth-century scientists limited themselves to the *how* without interest in the *why*. By and large, this is not true. Newton, like other early scientists, had no problem with the *why* because he began with the existence of a personal God who had created the universe. In fact, in his later years Newton wrote more about the Bible than about science, though little was published.

Newton, therefore, had no intention of "deifying" nature. He was engaged in more commonplace occupations: noting the effect which an ordinary glass prism had upon rays of light which passed through it; determining whether the deflection of the moon's orbit, at any minute of the moon's progress, was the same as the distance which a body at that height would move in the first minute of its fall toward the earth. Newton, however, struck the imagination of his time as Charles Darwin did of his time, just because his important conclusions were arrived at by such commonplace methods.

If the character of so intangible a thing as light could be discovered by playing with a prism and if, by looking through a telescope and doing a sum in mathematics, the force which held the planets could be identified by the force that made an apple fall to the ground, there seemed to be no end to what might be definitely known about the universe. Perhaps God moved in these clear ways to perform His wonders. And He had apparently given man a mind ingeniously fitted to discover these ways. Newton, more than any man before him, so it seemed to the eighteenth century, banished mystery from the world. In his hands philosophy came to be more than a matter of observation and mathematics. It became an occupation which any intelligent person might in some measure pursue, instead of the manipulation of a subtle dialectic which only the adept could follow and which created more difficulties than it solved.

The interest of the scientific world in Newton's work is indicated by the appearance, prior to 1789, of some eighteen editions or reprintings of the *Principia*.[6] This work literally filtered throughout Europe and found its way to America.

Significantly, Newton's fame was not confined to the scientific community. It was not necessary to read the *Principia* in order to be a good Newtonian, any more than it is necessary to read *Origin of Species* in order to be a good Darwinian. As Carl Becker notes:

> Relatively few people read the *Principia,* which contains much difficult mathematics. No less a person than Dr. Richard Bentley wrote to Newton for a list of books on mathematics by the aid of which he could study the *Principia* intelligently; and John Locke, himself no mean philosopher, had to take the word of Huygens that the mathematical parts of the book were sound. "Very few people read Newton," said Voltaire, "because it is necessary to be learned to understand him. But everybody talks about him." These people could subscribe to the Newtonian philosophy without ever having to open the formidable *Principia;* and they were well aware that the great scientist had uncovered the secrets of Nature, and of Nature's God, in a way that, to an earlier generation, might have seemed almost indiscreet. They were indoctrinated into the new philosophy through conversation, and through popular lectures and books which humanely omitted the mathematics of the *Principia,* devoting the space thus gained to a confident and edifying amplifi-

cation of its cautious conclusions which might have aston-
ished Sir Isaac himself, but which made the new philosophy
interesting and important to the average man.[7]

Added to this phenomenon is the fact that the colonial mind
had a peculiar respect and affinity for science. The opening of
America to settlement and the birth of modern science were
cognate developments of Western civilization. Science, with its
philosophical corollaries, was one of the most important intellectual forces shaping the destiny of eighteenth-century America. In
fact, colonial influence on English and European thought scored
its one modest success in the field of science.

Science in colonial America was not just science but Newtonian science, an inquiry into the phenomenon of the natural
world and the spirit with the methods of Isaac Newton. The
influence of Newton in America, which extended well beyond
the bounds of science, was a determining element in the relationships of the colonial mind to the world about it. Through Newton's writings the whole new approach to nature of Bacon, Co-
pernicus, Harvey, Kepler, Brahe, Galileo, Descartes, and Boyle
was impressed on colonial minds. And since Newton insisted
stubbornly that he had come not to destroy but to fulfill the
teachings of the revealed Christian religion, Cotton Mather
could take him to his bosom no less warmly than Benjamin
Franklin or other colonial thinkers.

Science in the colonies was divided into two broad categories: natural philosophy, in which physics and astronomy were the
most important special fields, and natural history, in which bot-
any aroused the keenest interest. Students of the colonial mind
need to use modern divisions and subdivisions of science with
extreme care, for the ideal of the whole man, certainly in the
field of science, still had meaning in the eighteenth century.

Key to understanding the influence of Newton is the fact
that the currents of science flowing in from England and Europe
and the freshets of science arising in the colonies gave a notable
swell to the onward cause of political liberty. The new freedom
in science and the new freedom of government were, of course,
collateral developments in the unfolding of the European Enlightenment as well as the colonial mind. It would be hard to say
which freedom, political or scientific, was more instrumental in
fostering the other. We may point to at least three ways in which

Newtonian science quickened the advance toward free government.

First, Newtonian science gave the concepts of an orderly, designed universe that was discoverable by use of reason. It not only fostered the concept that man by use of science could discover the truths of God's handiwork, but it also fostered the concept that government, like the laws of nature, could be an orderly system designed to promote freedom. Thus, a "decisive majority of the best minds in eighteenth-century America considered the use of reason an essential prop of free government, and science had done as much as any other intellectual force to advertise the beauties of reason to their minds."[8]

Second, the advance of science popularized other methods and assumptions that were essential to the conduct of free government. Many colonial minds began to recognize the kinship of the scientific method and democratic procedure. Free inquiry, free exchange of information, optimism, self-criticism, pragmatism, objectivity—all these ingredients of the coming American republic were already active in the republic of science that flourished in the eighteenth century.

Finally, the new science had a direct influence on the development of American political and constitutional thought. Basic to the Newtonian system were the great generalizations of a universe governed by immutable natural laws and of harmony as the pattern and product of these laws. The first of these gave new sanction to the doctrine of natural law; the second had much to do with the growing popularity of the Whiggish principle of balanced government. Clinton Rossiter writes:

> It is going a bit too far to look upon the American Constitution as a monument to Sir Isaac Newton, but certainly the widespread acceptance of his theory of a harmonious universe helped create an intellectual atmosphere in which a system of checks and balances would have a special appeal to constitution-makers. If John Winthrop could thank an immortal Newton for discovering the law of attraction and repulsion, "the fundamental law which the alwise Creator had established for regulating the several movements in this grand machine," certainly John Adams could thank him for supporting the law of checks and balances, the fundamental law of the machine of constitutional government.[9]

Of course, we must not overstate either the progress or influence of colonial science. America produced no Newton or Boyle, and science was but one of many intellectual forces that encouraged men to think in terms of human liberty. Yet we cannot ignore the influence of the scientific spirit in generating an attitude of optimism and open-mindedness, an attitude that the clergy preached and almanacs and newspapers helped to spread among the colonial people.

THE STATE OF NATURE

Another important concept shaping the colonial mind was the idea of a state of nature. This notion came to European thinking through classical philosophers like Seneca (3 B.C.-65 A.D.), a Roman Stoic, but primarily through the early church fathers.[10] The latter located "their primitive polity in the Garden of Eden before the Fall."[11] In other words, there existed, before the fall of Adam, an ideal state of community between men where human government was unnecessary.

The state of nature—in Lockean terms the state of men living together according to reason without a common superior on earth with authority to judge between them—became an important point of reference around which revolutionary thinkers grouped the principles of their political theory.

Arguing against governmental tyranny from the point of view of a state of nature was, at least, a good practical strategy. If, because of bad government, men had a right to return to a "pure" state of nature where there was no civil government, then all human governments had cause for alarm. As such, all governments could be divested of their power once the people opted to return to the state of nature.

Reflecting the colonial mind, Reverend Samuel Cooke elaborated upon the state of nature:

> In a pure state of nature, government is in a great measure unnecessary. Private property in that state is inconsiderable. Men need no arbiter to determine their rights; they covet only a bare support; their stock is but the subsistence of a day; the uncultivated deserts are their habitations, and they carry their all with them in their frequent removes. They are each one a law to himself, which, in general, is of force sufficient for their security in that course of life.
>
> It is far otherwise when mankind are formed into collec-

tive bodies, or a social state of life. Here, their frequent mutual intercourse, in a degree, necessarily leads them to different apprehensions respecting their several rights, even where their intentions are upright. Temptations to injustice and violence increase, and the occasions of them multiply in proportion to the increase and opulence of the society. The laws of nature, though enforced by divine revelation, which bind the conscience of the upright, prove insufficient to restrain the sons of violence, who have not the fear of God before their eyes.[12]

The true state of nature, therefore, was simply the condition of no positive (written) law and no formal government that preceded the organization of the political community. Locke theorized that it was a state of peace, goodwill, mutual assistance, and preservation. Moreover, recognizing the fall of the nature of man, the state of nature, like natural man, had much in it that was good, but also much that was bad.

The state of nature served as a logical antecedent to at least five major principles of revolutionary theory. It permitted the colonists, as Clinton Rossiter notes:

[To] (1) proclaim the prior existence and therefore prior validity of the law of nature, the system of natural justice that commands men to love, assist, and respect one another. . . . (2) describe man's basic nature, by calling attention to those qualities of character he possesses before and despite government or society. . . . (3) describe man's basic rights, which are therefore considered the gifts of God or nature and not of the community. . . . (4) demonstrate the clear necessity of government based on principles of freedom. . . . (5) give a mechanistic explanation of the origin of government, in order to free men from the past and let them build new political institutions to suit themselves.[13]

For men anxious to revert to first principles of natural justice, the state of nature was a prime philosophical assumption. "The dictates of a political theory concerned with limits on political power in behalf of individual liberty demanded that men and their rights be declared logically and chronologically anterior to the organized community."[14]

THE LAW OF NATURE

The Declaration of Independence was written, the Constitution adopted, and the republic launched in an age when most men, whether subtle or simple, believed "unequivocably in higher law."[15] In those days, the higher law was a curious mixture of biblical precepts and "the law of nature." As we have seen, most of the clergy saw the law of nature as being merely an expression of biblical maxims. Even those men who were skeptical of both the clergy and some biblical notions assumed the existence and applicability of "the Laws of Nature and of Nature's God":

> Thinking colonists realized that they were the latest heirs of a political tradition unrivaled in age and universality. By the time the law of nature had come into their hands, it had assumed many different shapes in the service of many different peoples and purposes. Greek philosophers, Roman jurists, Church fathers, medieval scholastics, Protestant reformers, Continental and English liberals—all these and many others had made rich contributions to the doctrine of natural law. And all had agreed, no matter what their special interpretation of its content and dictates, that it placed some sort of moral restriction on political power, indeed on all human activity.[16]

To be specific, colonial opinion of the ultimate source of higher law divided into several fairly distinct categories, although at times there was a strange mixture of these categories. One group of men held the higher law to be of immediately divine origin.

> For them the higher law was, as Rev. Eliphalet Williams of Hartford told the Connecticut legislature, "the law of God, eternal and immutable." New England preachers, at least the more conservative of them, were the leading members of this group, but it was by no means confined to clerical thinkers. James Otis, for example, considered the law of nature to be "the *unchangeable will of God,* the author of nature, whose laws never vary." For most of these thinkers, if not necessarily for Otis, the commands of the higher law were to be found primarily in Scripture. Since the great men of Israel had commanded a variety of things, Eliphalet Williams's law

of God was just about as flexible as Samuel Adams's law of nature.[17]

A second group sought, in the tradition of Cicero (106-43 B.C.) and Hugo Grotius (1583-1645), to place reason and biblical constructs on an equal footing in formulating their concept of the higher law. In somewhat of a deistic sense, God was moved further into the background. God became a distant observer. Such rationalists in religion were willing to concede that God had set the grand machine of nature in motion, but they added quickly that the laws governing this machine had by now become "natural."

One must note, however, that the great majority of these men, including Thomas Jefferson, were not deists in the true sense of the word. In fact, Jefferson was adamant in his belief in a theistic God who intervened in the course of history.[18] Basically, however, reason held its own with biblical revelation as a means of discovering the dictates of the higher law. The Newtonian influence is evident here.

Generally, in their speeches and writings, the colonists revealed the derivative quality of their political theory by quoting English and Continental definitions of the law of nature rather than seeking to totally define it for themselves. Locke and others were called into service for this purpose.

However, Sir William Blackstone's definition of the law of nature was probably the best known and most widely cited. Blackstone had been influenced by Lockean and Newtonian ideas. As professor Donald Lutz notes: "Blackstone himself cites Locke a number of times, and certain of his institutional and procedural concepts seem to be grounded in Locke insofar as they are congruent with Locke's principles, or logically implied by Locke."[19]

Blackstone's impact on the colonial mind was great.[20] No young man in America after 1771 could become a lawyer without reading Blackstone and maybe not without reading these words:

> Man, considered as a creature, must necessarily be subject to the laws of his Creator, for he is entirely a dependent being. . . . And consequently, as man depends absolutely

upon his Maker for every thing, it is necessary that he should in all points conform to his Maker's will.

This will of his Maker is called the law of nature. For as God, when He created matter, and endued it with a principle of mobility, established certain rules for the perpetual direction of that motion; so, when He created man, and endued him with freewill to conduct himself in all parts of life, He laid down certain immutable laws of human nature, whereby that freewill is in some degree regulated and restrained, and gave him also the faculty of reason to discover the purport of those laws.

Considering the Creator only as a being of infinite *power*, He was able unquestionably to have prescribed whatever laws he pleased to his creature, man, however unjust or severe. But as He is also a being of infinite *wisdom*, He has laid down only such laws as were founded in those relations of justice, that existed in the nature of things antecedent to any positive precept. These are the eternal, immutable laws of good and evil, to which the Creator Himself in all His dispensations conforms; and which He has enabled human reason to discover, so far as they are necessary for the conduct of human actions. Such among others are these principles: that we should live honestly, should hurt nobody, and should render to everyone his due; to which three general precepts Justinian has reduced the whole doctrine of law. . . . This law of nature, being coeval with mankind and dictated by God Himself, is of course superior in obligation to any other. It is binding over all the globe in all countries, and at all times: no human laws are of any validity, if contrary to this; as such of them as are valid derive all their force, and all their authority, mediately or immediately, from this original.[21]

For the colonist, the law of nature had at least four basic applications or meanings in colonial political theory. First, it was a set of moral standards governing private conduct. It was, in actuality, an expression of the Golden Rule. Derived from the Bible, it was held that men are to love their neighbors as themselves and to act and treat others as they would want to be treated themselves.

Second, the law of nature formed a system of abstract justice to which the laws of men should conform. Therefore, it was held that any law that ran counter to a community's inherent sense of right and wrong was not only a bad law but was no law at all.

Third, the law of nature formed a line of demarcation around the proper sphere of political authority. "Governments that pushed beyond it did so at peril of resistance or even revolution. Since the greatest and freest of constitutions was an earthly replica of natural law, any violation of it was both unconstitutional and unnatural."[22] This was Locke's message: that government must respect the commands of natural law or release men from obedience.

Finally, the law of nature was the source of natural rights. A truly free people, the colonists believed, would claim their rights as derived from the "Laws of Nature and of Nature's God" and not as a gift of the government or of the community. "In the final reckoning, natural law came to be equated with natural rights."[23]

By the time of the Revolution, the law of nature was a universally accepted article of faith. As a consequence, the "mind of God as read by revelation, the plan of nature as analyzed by right reason, and the history of mankind as interpreted by the scholars of the nation all proclaimed the reality of *moral* limits on political power."[24]

THE NATURE OF MAN

Revolutionary theorists devoted special attention to the exact nature of man. This is obviously where the clergy had an immense impact. Their sermons and pamphlets are full of assumptions and comments about the natural virtues and vices of the men about them.

There were, however, essentially several general attitudes as to the nature of man. Again, these attitudes comingle and intermix at different points. One small group of thinkers took the so-called "enlightened" view, considering man a naturally good, decent, friendly, capable person whose troubles were the bitter fruit of a world he had never made. Another, to which the clergy belonged, preached the doctrine of sin and depravity, preferring to lay stress on the tendency of man to do evil. However, as Rossiter notes, most "thinkers settled down, or oscillated, between these two extremes, finding much that was good and much that was bad in the character of every single man."[25]

Colonial thinkers in their writings recognized, therefore, that man had both good and bad qualities. Perhaps the most politically significant of all these qualities was "sociability." This is the urge man feels to associate with other men, even if this means surrendering a substantive part of his original freedom. Although most colonial thinkers believed in a state of nature that preexisted civil government, it was also believed that government and society were "natural" for the simple preservation of man himself. It seems, however, that the most thoughtful of the colonists made a distinction between society and government. "The former was the 'natural' result of the presence of a number of men in a certain area; the latter was the mechanistic if inevitable result of an act of will. In short, *the contract in Revolutionary thought was governmental, not social.*"[26]

A quality of man deserving special mention was the transformation that is more than likely to come over man when he is placed in a situation of power. The colonial thinkers tended to believe that man's fondness for power naturally led him to abuse it when he had acquired it.

> "Every man by nature," echoed Rev. Thomas Allen of Pittsfield, "has the seeds of tyranny deeply implanted within him." Although this belief in man's love of power was not nearly so strong or widely advertised as it was later to be in Federalist political theory, few authors failed to mention it as a human characteristic, and none went out of his way to deny it specifically. The universal American belief in constitutionalism and the rule of law—indeed in the necessity of a written, comprehensible constitution—derived from this suspicious appraisal of man in authority.[27]

Recognizing the fallen nature of man, the colonists sought two types of collective action to ennoble and assist man in life. These were "establishing or encouraging institutions, especially religious and political institutions, that would give free play to his [man's] virtues while controlling or supressing his vices; educating him to recognize the sweet harvest of the one and bitter fruits of the other."[28] It was believed that through education, aided by religion in the schools, man could learn to cherish virtue and shun vice. He could also learn how to serve the community and defend liberty. It is believed that free government rested on virtue, virtue on knowledge, and knowledge on regular techniques of education.

This eventually led to the public education system in the United States, which in its early form included the teaching of religion. Education, and in particular education in religion, remained a high priority throughout early American history. For example, the Northwest Ordinance of 1787, which set aside federal property in the territory for schools and was passed again by Congress in 1789 (the same Congress that wrote the United States Constitution), states the purpose of those schools: "Religion, morality, and knowledge being necessary to good government and the happiness of mankind, schools and the means of learning shall forever be encouraged." The sequence is significant: "religion" before morality, and that before knowledge. Religion as used here is the teaching of Christian ethics, the definition of religion of that time.

Even Thomas Jefferson, often cited as being hostile to religion, promoted its use in education. As founder of the University of Virginia he recommended that students be allowed to meet on the campus to pray and worship together, or if need be, to meet and pray with their professors on campus.[29] As author of the first plan of public education adopted for the city of Washington, D.C.,[30] he included the Bible and the *Isaac Watts Hymnal* as principal books to teach reading to students.[31]

Finally, it was held that the natural character of man was an alloy of virtue and vice. His natural state was pure freedom and equality. "Men might be grossly unequal in appearance, talents, intelligence, virtue, and fortune, but to this extent at least they were absolutely equal: No man had any natural right of dominion over any other; every man was free in the sight of God and plan of nature."[32]

There were two aspects of the doctrine of natural equality to which most colonial thinkers subscribed. They taught that equality among men existed within a limited sphere; within this sphere all men were created absolutely equal. Therefore, each man had an equal claim to be free of any earthly power and each could be governed only with his consent.

However, as the colonists were prone to pragmatism in their use of ideas and words, equality, in the end, took on an eclectic "national" sense. The Declaration of Independence affirmed that it was "necessary" for the United States "to assume among the powers the separate and equal station to which the Laws of Nature and of Nature's God entitles them." Historian Eugen Rosenstock-Huessy has noted this meaning:

The colonies desired equality with the motherland. The French word *égalité,* the rallying-cry of 1789, meant equality within one country. Equal the citizen should be, regardless of vocation or profession. The American word equality, in 1776, was much less individualistic. The whole body politic of the colonies was jealous of the pretensions of the body politic at home. The colony of Massachusetts called itself the Commonwealth of Massachusetts; the name United States recalled the United Kingdom. George Washington could be compared with the noblest and best type of English gentleman. The American state papers were written in a peerless style of parliamentary English. The content of the American Revolution was no novelty, no new discovery of the nature of man; it was, first of all, an assertion of the *equal* right of the pioneers to have their English way in the new world.

The inferiority complex of many educated Americans has its counterpart in the epoch of independence; the unquestioned leadership of Europe is to give way to an equality of the new States with the old Monarchies, or, as the Preamble of the Declaration says, "an equal station among the Powers of the Earth." This Equality of 1776, still belongs to the Anglo-Saxon world of values; whereas the *Egalité* of 1789 was a radical out-cry of men's individual nature.

The first version of Equality had been: We, the colonies, are the peers of the motherland. The second version, eleven years later, took cognizance of the tremendous universality of every word that is uttered by human faith.[33]

As such, independence meant, not isolation from the world, but the "equality" of America as an independent sovereign within the family of nations. In these terms, the colonists believed, the rights of the colonies could be secured from interference.

THE NATURAL RIGHTS OF MAN
The doctrine of natural rights was the hard core of revolutionary political theory. As noted, the natural rights of man were equated with natural law itself. "The rights of man, that is to say, not only depended upon or sprang from natural law; they *were* natural law, at least so far as it could be understood by men."[34]

By natural rights the colonists meant simply those rights which belonged to man as man. They used several adjectives in addition to "natural" to express the special qualities of these rights. They were natural, traceable directly to the great plan of nature as derived from the great Creator of the universe. These rights were, then, absolute, eternal, essential, and unalienable. "Inherent, universal, unalterable, inestimable, sacred, indefeasible, fundamental, inprescriptible, divine, God-given, hereditary, and indelible were other adjectives used to stamp the natural rights of mankind with transcendent significance."[35]

Although some colonial theorists seemed confused on this point, natural rights were, as they argued, different from civil or constitutional rights because natural rights belonged to man in a state of nature. He had brought them with him into society. He had also brought them with him into civil government.

Fundamental was the belief that man would take natural rights with him should he ever return to the state of nature or of a natural society. Thus, it is a basic article of the American dream that every man—no matter what his station, calling, learning, and fortune—had certain natural, unalienable rights.

The sources of natural rights were the sources of natural law: God and nature. Some colonial theorists were willing to merge God and nature into one magnificent and consecrated source. However, most would have agreed with John Dickinson (1732-1808):

> Kings or parliaments could not *give* the *rights essential to happiness*. . . . We claim them from a higher source—from the King of kings, and Lord of all the earth. They are not annexed to us by parchments and seals. They are created in us by the decrees of Providence, which establish the laws of our nature. They are born with us; exist with us; and cannot be taken from us by any human power, without taking our lives. In short, they are founded on the immutable maxims of reason and justice.[36]

In like manner, Alexander Hamilton (1757-1804) could say: "The Sacred Rights of Mankind are not to be rummaged for among old parchments or musty records. They are written, as with a sunbeam, in the whole volume of human nature, by the Hand of the Divinity itself, and can never be erased or obscured by mortal power."[37]

LIFE, LIBERTY, PROPERTY, HAPPINESS, AND CONSCIENCE
Certain rights were singled out as the legitimate possession of all men everywhere. They were life, liberty, property, conscience, and happiness.

The right to *life* was so far above dispute that colonial authors were content merely to mention it in passing. The strategic importance of the right to life lay in its great corollary or defense: the law or right of self-preservation. "This secondary right made it possible for a single man or a whole nation to meet force with force, to resist all arbitrary invasions of life, liberty, and property."[38]

Moreover, life is listed first in those "unalienable" rights mentioned in the Declaration of Independence. The right to life is the starting point for all other rights. Likewise, a nation that does not protect the right to life will, in the end, protect no rights at all.

The natural right to *liberty* was essential to all other rights. Indeed, a man without natural liberty was a contradiction in terms. "The God who gave us life," wrote Thomas Jefferson to George III, "gave us liberty at the same time."[39] Liberty was defined as the freedom and power of each individual to act as he pleased without restraint or control. From this natural liberty, the freedom from obligation to obedience, flowed all the other liberties that men enjoyed in society.

Essentially, the natural right to liberty became the right to be left alone to pursue one's own destiny. When, for instance, government became "important" or oppressive enough, the colonists found ways other than politics to express their wishes and to influence action. Sullen resistance, riots, and "going out west" are not generally recommended as effective techniques of political freedom in the modern era, but in colonial times they served a very real purpose.

Later, after independence and victory were assured over Great Britain, the right to liberty was reflected in America's first "constitution," the Articles of Confederation. The right to be left alone created, in essence, the Articles as such a tenuous governing document that a new constitution had to be drafted. It came about in 1789 in Philadelphia. It, too, left a great amount of freedom to the individuals and the states, even in the face of the formation of a federal government. Modern Americans—so accustomed to regulation and control—have trouble even conceiving how limited these documents were. But the colonial mind understood freedom in its natural state.

The right to acquire and enjoy *property* was universally acclaimed in the literature of the Revolution. Although John Locke had several times used the word "property" in the broad sense of everything a man is or has, the colonists usually limited their definition to ownership of things tangible or at least convertible to money. "Property in this sense was so essential to the fulfillment of man's promise and powers that it could almost be equated with liberty itself. If Locke included liberty in his definition of property, colonists included property in their definition of liberty."[40]

This is not because Americans were more materialistic than other people. Quite to the contrary, their primary, long-range concern was with the political and spiritual aspects of human freedom. "But the crisis of the moment, to which their theorizing was directed, was an unprecedented invasion of the right to dispose of property without compulsion: that is, the right of men to be taxed only by representatives of their own choosing."[41] This equated to being against taxation without representation and without consent.

Only two other rights—the right of conscience and the right of happiness—were ever placed by more than one or two authors at the same level of sanctity and universality with life, liberty, and property.

The right to *happiness*—or at least to pursue happiness without interference—was a logical assumption in the political theory of men of the colonial era.[42] The phrase "pursuit of happiness," which is found in the Declaration of Independence, was probably suggested by William Blackstone's statement that the law of nature boils down to "one paternal precept, 'that man should pursue his own true and substantial happiness.' "[43] Through all the writings of men like James Wilson, Richard Henry Lee, Thomas Jefferson, James Iredell, and clergymen such as Reverend Jonathan Mayhew runs a firm belief that God had surely willed the happiness of His creatures and that God did not make men to be unhappy. As John Dickinson put it:

> It would be an insult on the divine Majesty to say, that He has given or allowed any man or body of men *a right to make me miserable.* If no man or body of men has *such a right,* I have a *right to be happy.* If there can be no happiness without freedom, I have a *right to be free.*[44]

The right of *conscience,* the right of each individual to reach out for God without interference or even assistance from other men, was naturally a prime interest to a people well on their way to full religious liberty. This right has its roots in the Reformation and such concepts as Martin Luther's concept of "the priesthood of believers." It eventually found its embodiment in the First Amendment to the United States Constitution.

THE RIGHT OF RESISTANCE

Because of the impending crisis with Great Britain, the colonists were forced to search for an extraordinary line of defense. They found it in the right of resistance to tyranny. The whole effort of American thinkers was finally directed to legalizing the extraordinary right of appealing to arms and, therefore, the right to resist governmental authority.

As we saw with the clergy, the voice of those advocating resistance sometimes became strident. Some even castigated nonresistants. James Otis proclaimed: "He that would palm the doctrine of unlimited passive obedience upon mankind—is not only a fool and a knave, but a rebel against common sense, as well as the laws of God, of Nature, and his Country."[45]

One striking factor concerning the colonial thinkers, however, was the essential conservatism in terms of handling the doctrine of resistance. For example, most writers insisted on discussing resistance as a community right. For the most part, then, American theorists devoted their attention to the causes and techniques of large-scale, public resistance to arbitrary power and ignored the unalienable right of the *individual* to defend his life, liberty, and property against illegal force. This is not to say that the colonists did not uphold the right to self-defense, but, at the insistence of the clergy, they were not establishing a system of vigilantes. This, again, illustrates that the right of lower magistrates to resist, as advocated in political Calvinism, had an impact on colonial thinking.

The American theorists were constitutionalists. Thus, they placed special emphasis on the broken contract as justification for community resistance. The will of God, as expressed in the Old and New Testaments, and natural law as well as the British Constitution, they argued, all sanctioned popular resistance to oppressive authority. The one clear occasion for exercising the right of resistance, however, was the breaking of the original contract, thus overleaping the bounds of the fundamental law. And with George III's breaking his contractual duties with the colonists, it became a duty that the governmental authority ought to be resisted.

Basic to any true understanding of the American Revolution is the fact that legally the American colonists were not under the authority of the British Parliament. The colonial charters were contracts between the founders of the colonies and the king. Parliament was not involved contractually. Moreover, it must be remembered that—unlike the French and Spanish colonies—twelve of the English colonies were settled by individuals without any aid from the king or Parliament.

All the charters, particularly those of the New England colonies, granted companies and proprietors full executive, legislative, and judicial authority. Parliament was not involved, and King George had only restraining power. The Rhode Island and Connecticut charters did not even involve the king. They were seen as contracts between the people and God. And any prolonged, oppressive violation of these charter-contracts meant resistance.

However, resistance to a legal authority, not rebellion or revolution, was the only right and purpose of the American colonists. Rossiter notes:

> The emphasis their spokesman placed on the broken contract permitted them to deny absolutely that they are rebellious in nature or revolutionary intent. It was all as simple as this: They had contracted away—not irrevocably—their original power to govern themselves. They were meeting the harsh fact of a major breach of the contract by resuming this power and granting it to others on new terms. The rulers who had exercised unlawful authority were the real rebels. The people were merely exercising "the right of saving themselves from ruin."[46]

Resistance to unlawful authority, to breaches of the original contract, was more than just a right or a virtue. It was argued by many that resistance to governmental authority was a "Christian and social duty of each Individual."[47] One colonial minister argued that "the man who refuses to assert his right to liberty, property, and life, is guilty of the worst kind of rebellion; he commits high treason against *God*."[48] Even further, "he is betrayer of generations yet unborn."[49]

American colonial theorists revealed their conservative orientation in other refinements or qualifications of the right to resistance. First, they rejected flatly the stock Tory argument that to admit the right of resistance was simply to invite political and social instability. Only after systematic abuse of authority was any type of resistance deemed appropriate. Resistance, as Jefferson said in the Declaration of Independence, was justified, in the Lockean phrase, only after "a long train of abuses."

Second, the people had a solemn duty to be peaceful and law-abiding. Resistance and force were to be used only as a last defense against tyranny.

Third, the nature and extent of resistance was to be determined by the nature and extent of oppression. Petty tyranny called for passive resistance. Premeditated despotism called for active resistance. Resistance in the extreme sense of outright revolution was never to be undertaken except by an overwhelming majority of a thoroughly abused people, and this only through their representatives.

Finally, nearly all colonial writers agreed with Jefferson's assumptions that any exercise of "the right of the people to alter or abolish" government would be followed almost immediately by an exercise of their associated right to "institute new government":

> Men did not revolt against government to eliminate it entirely and return to a state of nature, but to organize a new one, "laying its foundation on such principles and organizing its powers in such form, as to them shall seem most likely to effect their Safety and Happiness." God granted men the right of resistance to help them preserve orderly constitutional government, not to induce them to fly from the tyranny of arbitrary power to the tyranny of no power at all.[50]

The natural God-given right of resistance to arbitrary power was the last resort of a people unable to protect their lives, liberties, and property by normal constitutional methods. It was a right to be exercised only by an overwhelming majority of the community, by way of their representatives, against rulers who had so completely ignored the terms of the original contract as to make further allegiance a crime against God and reason.

The people could be counted on never to resist except under overwhelming compulsion and to temper their methods to the nature and degree of oppression. The only possible outcome of the full reversion of power to the people was a new contract with new rulers under new terms of reciprocal protection and allegiance.

Resistance or revolution was not so much the right as the solemn, unpleasant duty of a betrayed people. In other words, never have a people engaged in revolution been so anxious to convince themselves and the world that they were not really revolutionaries at all—at least in the modern sense.

PART THREE

SACRED AND SECULAR

Secularism . . . is the name for an
ideology, a new closed world view
which functions very much like a
new religion. . . . It is a closed
ism. It menaces . . . openness and
freedom. . . . [I]t must therefore be
watched carefully to prevent its
becoming the ideology of a new
establishment. It must be
especially checked where it
pretends not to be a world view
but nonetheless seeks to impose
its ideology through the organs of
the state.

Harvey Cox (1966)

NINE

A NEW ORDER
FOR THE AGES

*I*t was not until the twentieth century, and particularly the 1940s onward, that there was any serious attempt to openly "secularize" American government. Secularization, in actuality, is the child of the twentieth century.

Secularism's children—Hitler, Stalin, Mao, Castro, and the like—found fertile ground in the concept of the secular state. In fact, the word *tyrant,* from the Greek *tyrannos,* means a secular ruler, one who rules without the sanction of religious law—an authority not derived from worship, or a power religion had not established. Unfortunately, we of modernity shudder in fear as we hope that the next secular tyrant can be checked before he or she is turned loose upon the world.

However, this was not a problem for the Americans of the eighteenth century. Society still clung to the belief in absolutes and the dignity of man. And when the rights of man were in any way infringed upon, protest and resistance followed. As we have seen, this sprang from a religious view of life in general.

CHURCHMEN

A popular myth is that the "founding fathers," or more properly, the framers, were essentially a nonreligious group who had in mind the secularization of American society and government. Nothing could be further from the truth.

The framers and early leaders were not all Christians. Most, however, could clearly be classified as "churchmen." This means they were regular attendants at a church, and some were actively involved in local church affairs. This fact should not come as a surprise, but in modern secular America it has been largely forgotten.

The author of the Declaration of Independence, Thomas Jefferson, although in his later life regarded by some as an "infidel," and certainly holding and advocating at times views quite inconsistent with those accepted by any traditional Christian, "served as a vestryman in his early days and was by birth and baptism connected with the Church."[1] William Stevens Perry writes: "To the very last of life he was a regular attendant at Church and must be classed, in view of his baptism, family associations, and lifelong attendance on the services of the Church, as, at least, a nominal Churchman. His Prayer-Book, used in Church in his latest years, is still preserved."[2]

The same holds true of the signers of the Declaration of Independence. "[T]hirty-four were Churchmen, while at least seven other Churchmen, eligible as signers by their actual votes in July for Independence or by their membership in August, were . . . hindered from giving their signatures" to the Declaration.[3]

The implication from affiliation with church and Christian organizations is that the framers and early leaders either were religious or held a religious view on life. This view was, in some instances, distinctly Christian and, in other instances, nominally derived from Christian teaching or simply a perversion of Christian beliefs. Combined with the influence of the clergy, this generally created a transcendent view of life and government in early America. Moreover, because of the decades of millenarian teaching before them, they approached the future with optimism.

ANNUIT COEPTIS

How religious this early leadership was can be seen at a glance of the reverse side of a United States one dollar bill. In the center is the motto, "In God We Trust," chosen as such by Congress during the presidency of Dwight D. Eisenhower. To the left and right are the two sides of the Great Seal of the United States, chosen by Congress two centuries earlier. On one side of the Great Seal there is an unfinished pyramid, symbol of the unfinished republic and its strength, above which there is an eye inside a triangle surrounded by rays of light, symbol of that divine favor in which the young nation placed its hope and confidence. This is made explicit in the Latin words just above the eye, adapted from Virgil's (70-19 B.C.) Aeneid—Annuit Coeptis, "He has favored our undertaking."

At the base of the pyramid are engraved Roman numerals for the year 1776, below which are emblazoned the words that announce the framers' belief in what they had actually done by way of God's favor: *Novus Ordo Seclorum,* "a new order for the ages." The original of this phrase is the guiding line of Virgil's Fourth Eclogue, a nativity hymn celebrating the world's salvation and the phenomenon of birth. Seeing the human species regenerating itself constantly and forever, Virgil had written: "The great order of the ages is born anew." The framers, however, believed that what they had done was not a "great" order of ages repeating itself, but a "new" order of the ages. Hence, the change in the wording. "The year 1776 marked for them the start of something different, an entirely new story never told before, an absolutely new beginning."[4]

The sense of a new beginning is strong. On July 4, 1776, before the day's work was ended, Congress appointed three of the committee that had drafted the Declaration of Independence (Jefferson, Franklin, and Adams) to devise a seal for the United States of America. It is characteristic of the background of the times that Franklin, Adams, Jefferson, and Du Simitiere, a French artist of Philadelphia who made the sketch for the committee, incorporated into the seal the eye of Providence. What these men wanted the Great Seal of the United States to symbolize is interesting. Benjamin Franklin suggested Moses standing on the shore depicting the crossing of the Red Sea. Thomas Jefferson proposed the children of Israel in the wilderness.[5]

The exodus of Israel from Egypt was for them a symbol of liberation and future freedom, as well as the conquest of a promised land. The basic reality in their life was the analogy of the children of Israel. They conceived that by going out into the wilderness they were reliving the story of the Exodus.

The American Revolution was, then, not only the foundation of a new body politic but also the beginning of a specific national history—"the first nation"—the first major colony to successfully break away through revolution from that colonial rule which was at the time everywhere taken for granted. "I always consider the settlement of America," wrote John Adams in 1765, "as the opening of a grand scheme and design in Providence for the illumination of the ignorant and the emancipation of the slavish part of mankind all over the earth."[6]

This sense of destiny is certainly not peculiar to Americans. It is an ingredient in the self-consciousness of every people who try to define their corporate sense of direction through history. However, as Christopher Mooney recognizes:

> What is peculiar to Americans is the interpretation given by the Founders to this formative experience: they translated it into the experience of Israel's exodus from Egypt. In other words, Americans were not just a rebellious people; they were a chosen people, whose subsequent history was to be built upon a faith experience.[7]

Those of Revolutionary America saw themselves participating in the building of a new millennium on earth, or what some may call a utopia. This fact, combined with the dominance of certain Christian beliefs in public life, led them to believe this to be a basis for a future hope.

REDEEMER NATION

Except in recent years, millennialism has been a strong current in the American psyche. Essentially it took the Civil War and the two world wars of the twentieth century to shake the belief that America's destiny was to establish God's Kingdom here on earth.

What follows is not an attempt to say that the millennial position is true either theologically or politically. To the contrary, the purpose in discussing millennialism is to paint an historically accurate picture (for better or for worse). In fact, as we note the pessimism of contemporary society, the millennial vision may have been illusion and the new order of the ages has become merely a secularized version of a past millennial hope.

Just at the turn of the century the statesman-historian Albert J. Beveridge, speaking in the United States Senate, stated the purpose and calling of the American nation as he saw it:

> God has not been preparing the English-speaking and Teutonic peoples for a thousand years for nothing but vain and idle self-contemplation and self-admiration. No. He made us master organizers of the world to establish a system where chaos reigned. He has given us the spirit of progress to overwhelm the forces of reaction throughout the earth. He has made us adept in government that we may administer government among savage and senile peoples. Were it not for such a force as this the world would relapse into barbarism

and night. And of all our race He has marked the American people as His chosen nation to finally lead in the redemption of the world.[8]

Here, in capsule form, are the elements of the idea historian Ernest Lee Tuveson has called "the redeemer nation."[9] Tuveson elaborates: "Chosen race, chosen nation; millennial-utopian destiny for mankind; a continuing war between good (progress) and evil (reaction) in which the United States is to play a starring role as world redeemer."[10]

As to how Americans came to view themselves as redeemers of the world in terms of a millennial hope, we must again look to the legacy of European history which America inherited. The crucial change came with the reversal of the Augustinian interpretation of history, which had prevailed during the Middle Ages and the Renaissance. Augustine assumed that the "City of God," the mystic body of the faithful, must live, usually subject to some degree of persecution, separate from the world of action until the "Last Judgment" would roll up history itself. As Tuveson writes:

> Although the Book of Revelation predicts that there will be a time when the power of evil is to be "bound"—the millennium—that prophecy is to be interpreted only allegorically; the millennium, Augustine concluded, began with the Resurrection. If the power of Satan is "bound" even in this age, with all its woes from mankind, then the outlook for mankind in this world can never be hopeful.[11]

Yet, even during the Middle Ages, isolated groups were never content with such an interpretation. As we saw earlier, with the outbreak of the persecution of Christians in the sixteenth and seventeenth centuries in Europe and the resultant resistance writings and actual resistance to authority, many began to see themselves in a totally different light. The idea of individualism was born, and the belief that the individual man could triumph over evil gave an entirely new perspective to what it meant to be a human being. Many began to see the Bible, both Old and New Testaments, as prophesying a glorious time when the kingdoms of this world would become in literal fact the Kingdom of God, when swords would be beaten into plowshares, when "the kingdom and dominion, and the greatness of the kingdom under the whole heaven, shall be given to the people of the saints of the most High, whose kingdom is an everlasting kingdom, and all dominions shall serve and obey him."[12]

In the light of such promises, was it reasonable to believe, with Augustine, that God had condemned His people to suffer under the heel of the wicked, to allow the creation which He had made so fair, originally, to be marred by the dominance of evil until the very end of time? May the prophesies of the Revelation not be literally true after all—may not God's plan envisage the step-by-step triumph of good over evil?

Only isolated and radical minorities, however, asked such questions until the Reformation began a whole new examination of Scripture. Even in the late sixteenth century some biblical scholars began to conclude that perhaps, after all, there was to be a millennium, a period in which Christ would rule. In the next century, however, the conception took a new and momentous turn. Maybe, as Augustine had thought, the Revelation should be taken partly in an allegorical sense—but with a very different significance. "Perhaps the millennium was to be an earthly *utopia,* an age at the end of all history, in which, not Christ in person, but Christians and Christian principles would really be triumphant. Human life would go on as before, but how much more happily! War would cease; poverty would be largely if not completely eliminated; knowledge would increase as never before; men would at least know true justice and mercy."[13]

Read in the light of this expectation, other biblical prophecies took on a new and revolutionary meaning. "The course of all history was seen as a great series of struggles, in which the Prince of Darkness is progressively defeated, according to a preconceived plan. The plan, moreover, was already far advanced; the interpreters generally felt that, with the Reformation, the turning point had been reached, and that the source of the evil had already received his death blow."[14] Tuveson writes:

How glorious the future would be! What a great part men living in the last days might play in bringing about the true utopia! Yet, it was frequently warned, great battles still lay ahead; the powers of evil were doomed to defeat, but their resources still were large, and the Revelation had predicted that Satan in his death pang could rage more strongly than ever before.[15]

In such a pattern of history, God would have to operate through certain nations. The old conception of a "chosen people," called to fight the battles of the Lord, was revived. Augustine had replaced the chosen people with the mystical conception of the hidden City of God. Now it would appear that God must use peoples, armies, and governments to obtain His ends. God had reentered history as a participant.

Many factors contributed to point to one people and one nation as chosen to perform God's work in the last days. It seemed as if the finger of Providence had pointed to the young republic of the West. The image was a popular one, with commentators taking literally the concept that America was a chosen nation. As Tuveson notes, it was not taken literally by a minority, but "by what seems to have been a majority of the Trinitarian Protestants of the United States."[16]

It should not be surprising then that President Woodrow Wilson could proclaim: "America had the infinite privilege of fulfilling her destiny and saving the world." Again, the vision for this concept, although altered by the time of Woodrow Wilson, was given to America by the clergy.

THE MILLENNIUM
The colonial sermons, if they were not always millennial, "contained a blueprint for the future as well as a record of the past."[17] As such, they could be labelled "millennial."[18] However, when such sermons were overtly millennial in character, they were dogmatic and pointed.

For example, in assessing the impending war between Great Britain and the American colonies, Reverend Samuel Sherwood proclaimed: "God Almighty, with all the powers of heaven, are on our side. . . . Great numbers of angels, no doubt, are encamping round our coasts, for our defence and protection. Michael stands ready, with all the artillery of heaven, to encounter the dragon, and to vanquish this black host."[19]

With a confidence almost prophetic, Sherwood announced the coming defeat of the "antichristian tyranny" which the British government represented. Because the king's chief minister had sipped "the golden cup of fornication" with "the old mother of harlots," they faced the imminent doom reserved for the wicked, persecuting tyrants of the earth.[20] In building the climax of his address, which translated the conflict into a struggle of cosmic significance, Sherwood predicted that the British attack on America was one "of the last efforts, and dying struggles of the man of sin."[21] From Sherwood's apocalyptic point of view America's victory would initiate Christ's millennial kingdom on earth.[22]

Sherwood was by no means the only American minister whose millennial hopes were fired by the revolutionary struggle. As Nathan Hatch notes:

> The cosmic interpretation of the conflict—God's elect versus Antichrist—appeared as a significant pattern in the intricate tapestry of ideas used by New England clergymen to explain the war's purpose. Moreover, by the time American victory seemed assured, the rhetoric of New England sermons was brimming with euphoric images of America's role in hastening the kingdom. The prospects for this blessed age had seemed so bright since the founding of New England. "Vice and immorality shall yet here, become . . . banished," proclaimed George Duffield, chaplain to the Continental Congress, "and the wilderness blossomed as the rose."[23]

Moreover, with "the coming of peace many ministers envisioned Christ's thousand-year reign on earth as an extension of the civil and religious liberty established in America."[24] Numerous clergy interpreted existing American society as the model upon which the millennial kingdom would be based. New England ministers of the Revolutionary era resisted tyranny in God's name, held liberty as the virtue of "New American Israel," and proclaimed that in sharing these values with all mankind America would become the principal seat of Christ's earthly rule.

Amid the shifting intellectual currents of eighteenth-century New England, one theme above all others maintained its hold on the clergy. It was the solid conviction that their community had been chosen as a special people of God. America had a special role to play in the scheme of providential history. Convinced that God had "planted a vine in this American wilderness" which He would "never suffer to be plucked up, or destroyed," and by visions of their own special place in a millennial kingdom, the clergy assumed this sense of identity which found its deepest support in the analogy between America and Old Testament Israel.

In this sense the past, as well as the future, was important. "The past was the tried-and-true key invariably invoked by ministers to interpret the present. Initially this past was largely limited to Israel's experience as recounted in the Old Testament which, New England colonists believed, was a 'type' or model for their own experience as God's 'New Israel.' "[25]

The assumption of the direct parallel between Israel and themselves ran deep. Hundreds of ministers chose Old Testament texts and applied them directly to the American colonies. Some made explicit typologies. Reverend Cyprian Strong, for example, explained in his sermon of 1777: "There is no one (I trust) whose mind is not at once struck with the description of Israel, as being a most perfect resemblance of these American Colonies: almost as much so, as if spoken with a primary reference to them."[26]

There was also a parallel drawn between what was occurring in the conflict with Great Britain and the Book of Revelation.

> With connotations even more evocative, numerous clergymen used the vivid imagery of the book of Revelation to define their own moral character vis-á-vis that of the British. The most common image of America, the fragile woman in the wilderness beset by the "malignant rages" of the red dragon, indicates that categories of Puritan providential history had not merely been reduced to "an overture to a stereotyped pattern." Instead, the Revolutionary decade produced as intense a biblical description of New England as any used since the original settlement of Massachusetts.[27]

Ebenezer Baldwin, who contracted a fatal disease during the British invasion of New York, had predicted as early as November 17, 1775, that the American colonies would be the "Foundation of a great and mighty Empire . . . which shall be the principal Seat of that glorious Kingdom, which Christ shall erect upon Earth in the latter Days."[28] Baldwin believed that the War for Independence was bringing on the final days because in America "the Principles of Liberty [were] to be better examined, than in the Foundation of any other Empire."[29] To Baldwin, America was freedom's last asylum and thus, despite gloomy military prospects, the center of God's redemptive plan.

Certainly the most striking feature of Revolutionary-era rhetoric is the way it adapted the framework of apocalyptic history to *political* ideas. Sermons during the war stressed repeatedly that American liberty was God's cause, that British tyranny was antichrist, and that sin was failure to fight the British.[30] With the coming of peace many ministers envisioned Christ's one thousand-year reign on earth as an extension of the civil and religious liberty established in America.[31] Hatch writes:

> This amalgam of traditional Puritan apocalyptic rhetoric and eighteenth-century political discourse I have chosen to call "civil millennialism," a term warranted by the extent to which these things were directed by the society's political consciousness. Under the aegis of civil millennialism ministers of varying theological persuasions came to homage at the same shrine, that of liberty, and expressed their allegiance in projections about the future which were as novel as they were persuasive.[32]

CIVIL MILLENNIALISM

With the great impact the clergy had on American society, it is little wonder that men like Franklin and Jefferson were proposing Old Testament symbols as appropriate for the Seal of the United States. Moreover, it was this civil millennialism preached by the New England clergy in the years prior to the American Revolution and afterward that led to the belief that America was a nation of destiny. Thus, the phrase "manifest destiny" came to mean that America's destiny was to be the light of the world and the chosen nation of God on earth. Even in its more secularized form, it lingers on in modern-day America. It is best expressed through the predominant civil religion of contemporary American culture.

A CIVIL RELIGION

While some have argued that Christianity is the national faith, "there actually exists alongside of and rather clearly differentiated from the churches [and Christianity] an elaborate and well-institutionalized civil religion in America."[1] This civil religion has come to characterize the consciousness of modern America and is a secularized counterpart to the traditional religion.

TRANSCENDENT REALITY
Roman Catholic teaching is determined by the church through its infallible pope and universal counsel. Traditional Protestantism appeals to an infallible Bible. What, then, shapes American civil religion?

"Originally," as Kenneth Kantzer writes, "no doubt, it [civil religion] took shape under strong Puritan influence, faced by the facts of colonial life."

> Not every New Englander was a Puritan separatist, and not every Virginian was a loyal Anglican. Yet they shared basic Judaeo-Christian convictions that they had inherited as part of Western culture. Puritans found them in the Bible; deists, in natural theology: All men and women are created in the image of God. Therefore, we must set high value on the personal integrity of every human. He or she must be respected, loved, protected, and served. Justice is due to all. We may persuade, but not coerce others so long as their actions are not destructive of the body politic and the rights of others.[2]

The political corollaries of these theological ideas became widely accepted by the Puritans of the eighteenth century. They were shared as part of the common faith by many American Protestants. "But they were also shared for the most part by Jews and deists (even Thomas Paine, and, of course, Thomas Jefferson). A century later, Roman Catholics were reluctantly admitted into the consensus. All shared a basic commitment to the Judeo-Christian value system, which served as the basis for political and social action, and thus for what has been called American civil religion."[3]

Robert Bellah defines civil religion as "that religious dimension, found I think in the life of every people, through which it interprets its historical experience in the light of transcendent reality."[4] Although American civil religion tends to be amorphous, it has certain basic convictions which have characterized it since its founding days:

> [G]overnment exists for the good of the citizens. Its duty is to seek their welfare, protect them, reward the innocent, and punish the guilty. Its ethical code is roughly comparable to the second table of the Decalogue, prohibiting stealing, adultery, murder, and false witness.
>
> Yet its powers are limited. Government has the right to manage the civil lives of its citizenry, but not their religious lives. All government is under God and his moral law. Every human being has political and social rights—in fact, equal rights before the law. All religion should be tolerated, and all religious practices—so long as they do not contradict public morality (variously defined). Democracy is the best form of government; and therefore, concern for others requires that we should extend it as far as possible by peaceful persuasion. Our part as citizens is to obey our government and respect it. We are to love our country and serve it.[5]

The civil religion then is those convictions and practices that determine the consciences and conduct of the people in terms of politics and general social structures. It deals with transcendent reality—that is, God—and, as we shall see, it displays the tenets of the American dream—rights, resistance, and future optimism—but without the depth previously provided by the older traditional religion. As such, civil religion is the tenuous cement that holds modern America together. Moreover, it can either serve the cause of freedom or become the tool of fascism or totalitarianism.

GOD AND COUNTRY

President John Kennedy's inaugural address of January 20, 1961, serves as an example and a clue with which to introduce the notion of America's civil religion. Kennedy stated:

> We observe today not a victory party but a celebration of freedom—symbolizing an end as well as a beginning—signifying renewal as well as change. For I have sworn before you and Almighty God the same solemn oath our forebears prescribed nearly a century and three quarters ago.
>
> The world is very different now. For man holds in his mortal hands the power to abolish all forms of human poverty and to abolish all forms of human life. And yet the same revolutionary beliefs from which our forebears fought are still at issue around the globe—the belief that the rights of man come not from the generosity of the state but from the hand of God.[6]

Kennedy concluded:

> Finally, whether you are citizens of America or of the world, ask of us the same high standards of strength and sacrifice that we shall ask of you. With a good conscience our only sure reward, with history the final judge of our deeds, let us go forth to lead the land we love, asking His blessing and His help, but knowing that here on earth God's work must be truly our own.[7]

There are three places in this brief address in which Kennedy mentions the name of God. Looking beyond this particular speech, we find that references to God are almost invariably to be found in the pronouncements of American presidents on solemn occasions, though usually not in the working messages that the president sends to Congress on various concrete issues. How are we to interpret these references to God? Moreover, considering the so-called separation of church and state, how is a president justified in speaking of *God* at all? The obvious answer is that the "separation of church and state" does not exclude religion from the political realm.

The inauguration of a president performs a significant symbolic function in the American civil religion. It affirms, among other things, the religious legitimation of the highest political authority. Let us look closely at what Kennedy actually said. First he said, "I have sworn before you and Almighty God the same solemn oath our forebears prescribed nearly a century and three quarters ago." The oath is the oath of office, including the acceptance of the obligation to uphold the Constitution. The president swears it before the people and God. Beyond the Constitution, then, the president's obligation extends not only to the people but to God. Kennedy's address, therefore, attributes a sovereignty to God. American civil religion has thus absorbed a key doctrine of traditional Christianity but, again, without the depth and meaning provided by the entire scope of Christian teaching.

Nevertheless, attributing sovereignty to God has important political implications concerning limitations on governmental power. Though the will of the people as expressed in the majority vote is carefully institutionalized as the operative source of political authority, it is deprived of an ultimate significance. In the civil religion, the "will of the people is not itself a criterion of right and wrong. There is a higher criterion in terms of which this will can be judged; it is possible that the people may be wrong. The president's obligation extends to the higher criterion."[8] This "higher criterion," though, is virtually never employed because of the egalitarianism that marks modern society. The president's propensity, as well as that of most politicians, is to seek the will of the people as expressed in polls and like devices. This explains the lack of statesmen in contemporary life and the fact that politicians, instead of statesmen, flourish in American government.

When Kennedy says that "the rights of man come not from the generosity of the state but from the hand of God," he is stressing the sovereignty of God again. As such, it does not matter whether the state is the expression of a will of an autocratic monarch or of the people. The "rights of man are more basic than any political structure and provide a point of revolutionary leverage from which any state structure may be radically altered. That is the basis of this reassertion of the revolutionary significance of America."[9]

Again, the impact of the preaching of the eighteenth-century clergy is still with us, albeit in secularized form. However, in its constitutional form it should, if properly argued and upheld, still provide protections for the people against the state.

The religious dimension in political life as recognized by Kennedy not only provides a grounding for the rights of man which makes any form of political absolutism illegitimate, but also provides a transcendent goal for the political process. This is implied in his final words that "here on earth God's work must truly be our own." This is more clearly explained in the previous paragraph of Kennedy's inaugural which has a distinctly biblical ring:

> Now the trumpet summons us again—not as a call to bear arms, though arms we need—not as a call to battle, though in battle we are—but a call to bear the burden of a long twilight struggle, year in and year out, "rejoicing in hope, patient in tribulation"—a struggle against the common enemies of man: tyranny, poverty, disease and war itself.[10]

This address can be understood only as a statement of an obligatory theme that lies very deep in the American tradition (and faintly resides in the American psyche and memory). The obligation is both collective and individual, and it is to carry out God's will on earth.[11] This was the motivating spirit of millennialism and of those who founded America, and has been present in every generation in some form or other.

Kennedy's inaugural also points to the religious aspect of the Declaration of Independence. There are four references to God in the Declaration of Independence. The first speaks of "the Laws of Nature and of Nature's God" which entitled any people to be independent. The second is the famous statement that all men "are endowed by their Creator with certain unalienable rights." Here Jefferson is obviously locating the fundamental legitimacy of the new nation in a conception of "higher law" that is itself based on both classical and natural law and biblical religion. The third is an appeal to "the Supreme Judge of the world for the rectitude of our intentions." The last indicates "a firm reliance on the protection of Divine Providence." These last two references imply a biblical God of history who stands in judgment over the world.

RELIGION AND CHRISTIANITY

The intimate relation of religious notions with the self-conception of the new republic is indicated by the frequency of their appearance in early official documents. For example, we find in George Washington's first inaugural address of April 30, 1789, such phrases as "Almighty Being who rules over the universe," "Invisible Hand," "smiles of Heaven," and so on.[12]

The words and acts of the framers, especially the first few presidents, shape the form and tone of the civil religion as it has been maintained ever since. However, as Robert Bellah remarks:

> Though much is selectively derived from Christianity, *this religion is clearly not itself Christianity.* For one thing, neither Washington nor Adams or Jefferson mentions Christ in his inaugural address; nor do any of the subsequent presidents, although not one of them fails to mention God. The God of the civil religion is not only "unitarian," he is also on the austere side, much more related to order, law, and right than to salvation and love. Even though he is somewhat deist in cast, he is by no means simply a watchmaker God. He is actively interested and involved in history, with a special concern for America.[13]

The Puritan influence—with its Calvinistic tinge—is evident at this point. Calvinism without an emphasis on "salvation and love" tends to drift toward the formation of a secular political doctrine. We saw this with the formation of political Calvinism, which, although Christian in influence, tended to go beyond the bounds of a spiritual Christianity. Thus, it translated logically from a personalized Christianity to a more aloof civil religion.

Also, the analogies drawn from the civil religion have much less to do with natural law or biblical law than with ancient Israel. The equation of America with Israel and the idea of "American Israel" is not infrequent throughout American history.[14] Moreover, what was implicit in the words of Washington already quoted becomes explicit in Thomas Jefferson's second inaugural address: "I shall need, too, the favor of that Being in whose hands we are, who led our fathers, as Israel of old, from their native land and planted them in a country flowing with all the necessaries and comforts of life."[15] Europe is Egypt. America is the Promised Land. God has, then, led His people to establish a new sort of social order that shall be the "light" unto all the nations. These ideas, of course, began with the colonial clergy and have now been absorbed into the civil religion.

What we have, thus, from the earliest years of the American republic is a collection of beliefs, symbols, and rituals with respect to "sacred" things and institutionalized in a collectivity. It is emphasized that the civil religion, while historically not directly and openly antithetical to and indeed sharing much in common with Christianity, "was neither sectarian nor in any specific sense Christian."[16]

There is, then, an evident *tension* between the civil religion and true Christian teaching. At a time when society was strongly influenced by Christianity (colonial America, for example), the emergence of the civil religion was believed to coincide with the basic beliefs of the Christian religion. Colonial America produced a common individual morality in a unique historical setting (which is no longer present). As such, that environment kept the tension from becoming intense. There are evidences, such as increased confrontations with the state and society by Christians and other religious persons, that the tension is now more acute.

At the same time, it is important to note that the civil religion was not, in the minds of such men as Franklin, Washington, Jefferson, or the other leaders (except for a few like Tom Paine), ever felt to be a substitute for Christianity.[17]

> There was an implicit but quite clear division of function between the civil religion and Christianity. Under the doctrine of religious liberty, an exceptionally wide sphere of personal piety and voluntary social action was left to the churches. But the churches were neither to control the state nor to be controlled by it. The national magistrate, whatever his private religious views, operates under the rubrics of the civil religion as long as he is in his official capacity, as we have already seen in the case of Kennedy.[18]

The framers seemed to view Christianity and the civil religion in parallel streams. Christianity was seen as the foundation of moral strength in the private realm. The civil religion, on the other hand, was the public acknowledgment of God and morality, minus such Christian doctrines as salvation, the depravity of man, and the concepts of heaven and hell, all which tend to divide men. An important function of the civil religion is, of course, unification of the people into a community. This function, as we shall see, can degenerate into statist authoritarianism.

Of all the principal framers-founders, Benjamin Franklin in style of life and public utterances may have been farthest from conventional piety. Some of the dogmas of the Presbyterian faith in which he had been raised, he wrote in his *Autobiography* (1789), "appeared to me unintelligible, others doubtful, and I early absented myself from public assemblies of the sect, Sunday being my study day."[19] When George Whitefield came to preach in Philadelphia in 1739, Franklin struck up a close friendship but resisted the evangelist's efforts to bring him to salvation. Said Franklin: "He us'd, indeed, sometimes to pray for my conversion but never had the satisfaction of believing that his prayers were heard. Ours was a mere civil friendship, sincere on both sides, and lasted to his death."[20]

Even Franklin, however, was convinced of the practical utility of Christianity. History, he wrote in his 1749 plan for educating the youth of Pennsylvania, shows "the Necessity of a *Publick Religion,* from its usefulness to the Publick; the Advantage of a Religious Character among private Persons, the Mischiefs of Superstition . . . and the excellency of the CHRISTIAN RELIGION above all others ancient or modern."[21] The great mass of men and women, he later observed, "have need of the motives of religion to restrain them from vice, to support their virtue, and retain them in the practice of it till it becomes habitual."[22] Here, again, Franklin was speaking of the Christian religion.

John Adams leaned toward rationalism. He never departed far, however, from the Puritan-Calvinistic belief that valid social law depends ultimately on religious sanction. "Statesmen may plan and speculate for Liberty," he wrote to Abigail, his wife, in 1775, "but it is Religion and Morality alone which can establish the principles upon which Freedom can securely stand. A patriot must be a religious man."[23]

THE CIVIL WAR

Until the American Civil War, the civil religion focused on the event of the Revolution, which was seen as the final act of the Exodus from the old lands across the waters. "The Declaration of Independence and the Constitution were the sacred scriptures and Washington the divinely appointed Moses who led his people out of the hands of tyranny."[24] The Civil War, which Sidney Mead calls "the center of American history," was the second great event that involved the national self-understanding so deeply as to require expression in the civil religion.[25]

The Civil War raised deep questions of national meaning. The man who not only formulated but in his own person embodied its meaning for America was Abraham Lincoln. For him the issue was not in the first instance slavery but "whether that nation, or any nation so conceived, and so dedicated, can long endure." He had said at Independence Hall in Philadelphia on February 22, 1861:

> All the political sentiments I entertain have been drawn, so far as I have been able to draw them, from the sentiments which originated in and were given to the world from this Hall. I have never had a feeling, politically, that did not spring from the sentiments embodied in the Declaration of Independence.[26]

The phrases of the Declaration of Independence constantly echo in Lincoln's speeches. Lincoln obviously saw his task as, first of all, to save the Union—not for America alone but for the "meaning of America" for the whole world for all time.

With the Civil War, a new theme of death, sacrifice, and rebirth enters the civil religion. It is symbolized in the life and death of Lincoln. Nowhere is it stated more biblically than in the Gettysburg Address, which has been called part of the Lincolnian "New Testament" among the civil scriptures.[27] Robert Lowell has pointed out the "insistent use of birth images" in this speech explicitly devoted to "these honored dead." The birth images, as Lowell notes, are also found in such phrases as "brought forth," "conceived," "created," and "new birth of freedom." He goes on to say:

> The Gettysburg Address is a symbolic and sacramental act. Its verbal quality is resonance combined with a logical, matter of fact, prosaic brevity. . . . In his words, Lincoln symbolically died, just as the Union soldiers really died—and as he himself was soon really to die. By his words, he gave the field of battle a symbolic significance that it had lacked. For us and our country, he left Jefferson's ideals of freedom and

equality joined to the Christian sacrificial act of death and
rebirth. I believe this is a meaning that goes beyond sect or
religion and beyond peace and war, and is now part of our
lives as a challenge, obstacle and hope.[28]

Important here is the shift from a Hebraic symbolism to a
"Christian" symbolism but without any sectarian implication.
The earlier symbolism of the civil religion had been Hebraic
without being in any specific sense Jewish.[29] The Gettysburg
symbolism—"those who here gave their lives, that that nation
might live"—is "Christian" without having anything specifically
to do with Christianity.

The symbolic equation of Lincoln with Jesus Christ was
made relatively early in the American civil religion. Lincoln's law
partner described him as "the noblest and loveliest character
since Jesus Christ. . . . I believe that Lincoln was God's chosen
one."[30]

With the Christian archetype in the background, Lincoln, as
a martyred president, was linked to the war dead, those who, in
his words, "gave the last full measure of devotion." The theme of
sacrifice was from here on indelibly written into the civil religion.

The new symbolism soon found both physical and ritualistic
expression. The great number of war dead required the establishment of a number of national cemeteries, the most famous being
the Arlington National Cemetery. It has subsequently become
one of the most hallowed monuments of the civil religion.

Memorial Day, which grew out of the Civil War, gave rich
expression to the things we have been discussing. The Memorial
Day observance, especially in the towns and smaller cities of
America, is a major event for the community involving a rededi-
cation to the martyred dead, to the spirit of sacrifice.[31] Moreover, as Bellah notes:

Just as Thanksgiving Day, which incidentally was securely
institutionalized as an annual national holiday only under the
presidency of Lincoln, serves to integrate the family into the
civil religion, so Memorial Day has acted to integrate the
local community into the national cult. Together with the
less overtly religious Fourth of July and the more minor
celebrations of Veterans Day and the birthdays of Washing-

ton and Lincoln, these two holidays provide an annual ritual calendar for the civil religion. The public-school system serves as a particularly important context for the cultic celebration of the civil religions.[32]

The civil religion has made an easy connection with the political realm. It is true that the relation between religion and politics in America has been singularly smooth (only to be brought into serious contention in modern secular society). As Alexis de Tocqueville wrote:

> The greatest part of British America was peopled by men who, after having shaken off the authority of the Pope, acknowledged no other religious supremacy: they brought with them into the New World a form of Christianity which I cannot better describe than by styling it a democratic and republican religion.[33]

Tocqueville further comments:

> In the United States even the religion of most of the citizens is republican, since it submits the truths of the other world to private judgement, as in politics the care of their temporal interests is abandoned to the good sense of the people. Thus every man is allowed freely to take that road which he thinks will lead him to heaven, just as the law permits every citizen to have the right of choosing his own government.[34]

It must be remembered that the churches opposed neither the Revolution nor the establishment of democratic institutions. Even when some of them opposed the full institutionalization of religious liberty, they accepted the final outcome with good grace. Part of the reason for this is that the American civil religion was never anticlerical or militantly secular. On the contrary, it borrows selectively from the religious tradition in such a manner that the average American sees no conflict between the two. In this way, "the civil religion was able to build up without any bitter struggle with the church powerful symbols of national solidarity and to mobilize deep levels of personal motivation for the attainment of national goals."[35]

"GOD"

The civil religion is obviously involved in the most pressing moral and political issues of the day. However, it is also caught in another kind of crisis, theoretical and theological, of which some are now becoming aware.

God has clearly been a central symbol in the civil religion from the beginning and remains so today. In the beginning, whether one stood on the left or the right, and regardless of church or sect, the idea of God was an accepted fact. The rapid rise of secularism in the twentieth century, however, has meant the demise of the concept of God and traditional religion. It is as if the very soul of the nation is being challenged.

The concept of the millennium or utopia as it was later seen in terms of the civil religion still looks for and holds hope for the future. However, the civil religion was never meant to be secular. As we saw, even those such as Thomas Jefferson and Benjamin Franklin, although holding up to a broad civil religion, professed that the Christian religion was the best source of private morals. This, they believed, was good for the populace and good for the nation.

It was inevitable, however, that once the civil religion lost its traditional Christian character, it would eventually serve secular goals and ends and eventually serve as the "church" over the nation. Moreover, with the attainment and entrenchment of the newly secularized civil religion and the demise of the private morals of Christianity, we have seen the demise of the American society. "Private" morality may soon become a vision of the past. This is true to such an extent that many see no future at all (as the suicide rate attests), and end-time scenarios are the picture of reality for the modern American.

As the secularized civil religion has become more pervasive and more public, the so-called "private" morality of Christianity has been privatized, thus eliminating its public significance. With the rise of secularism and its trend toward "closing out" all manifestations of supernatural religion, privatization of religion has become a major concern. As professor Harold Berman has noted: "The significant factor in this regard . . . has been the very gradual reduction of the traditional religions to the level of a personal, private matter, without public influence on legal development, while other belief systems—new secular religions ('ideologies,' 'isms')—have been raised to the level of passionate faiths for which people collectively are willing not only to die but also . . . to live new lives."[36]

As a result, traditional Christianity has lost much of its public character as well as its political influence. Says Berman: "For the most part, people go to church as individuals, or as individual families, to gain spiritual nourishment to sustain them in activities and relationships that take place elsewhere. . . . We are thus confronted with a combination of a 'religionless Christianity' in what may be called a 'Christianity-less religion.' "[37] Thus, Christianity and other religions become more and more restricted to the private realm and therefore lose their public manifestations.

A dangerous aspect of the civil religion is its attempt to unify the nation as a collective. As the people of America become less diversified, the civil religion has the power to engender the masses to propaganda. With the "right" leader or leaders, the American people could be moved (and this is not farfetched) to make war or peace in the name of some less than worthy ideal. As history has taught us, the masses can be moved to approve of atrocities in the name of love of their country and their civil religion. Nazi Germany is an obvious example.

In fact, the German people actually welcomed Hitler. We must not forget that the Nazi party was elected to office, under a constitutional government, by freely cast ballots of millions of German voters, including people on every social, economic, and educational level.

On January 30, 1933, in full accordance with the country's legal and constitutional principles, Hitler was appointed chancellor. When German President Hindenburg died in August 1934, Hitler assumed the office of president as well as that of chancellor, but he preferred to use the title *Der Füehrer* (the leader) to describe himself. This new move was approved in a general election in which Hitler obtained 88 percent of the votes cast.[38]

Finally, as we have lost our sense of absolutes, the distinctions between what is good and what is bad has been blurred. As Robert Bellah has noted: "It is one of the oldest of sociological generalizations that any coherent and viable society rests on a common set of moral understandings about good and bad, right and wrong, in the realm of individual and social action. It is almost as widely held that these common moral understandings must also in turn rest upon a common set of religious understandings that provide a picture of the universe in terms of which the moral understandings make sense. Such moral and religious understandings produce both a basic cultural legitimization for a society which is viewed as at least approximately in accord with them and a standard of judgment for the criticism of a society that is seen as deviating too far from them."[39]

In colonial America and on through the nineteenth century, there was a common set of religious and moral understandings rooted in a conception of divine order under at least a nominally Christian God. The basic moral norms that were seen as deriving from that divine order were liberty, justice, and charity. These were understood in a context of theological and moral discourse which led to a concept of personal virtue as the essential basis of a good society. However, as Bellah notes: "How far we have come from that common set of understandings is illustrated by the almost negative meaning of the word 'virtue' today."[40]

Moreover, in an age when secular technology views man as nothing but a consumer and a cog in the great machine of technology, it is essential that we recover the dignity of people and the freedom to move within American traditional moral guidelines.[41] Again, as Bellah has astutely recognized, "only a new imaginative, religious, moral, and social context for science and technology will make it possible to weather the storms that seem to be closing in on us in the late 20th century. I am convinced that the continued and increased dominance of the complex of capitalism, utilitarianism, and the belief that the only road to truth is science will rapidly lead to the destruction of American society, or possibly in an effort to stave off destruction, to a technical tyranny of the 'brave new world' variety."[42]

Therefore, no matter how strong the glue of the civil religion or no matter how endearing it may be to the American people, the passionate loyalty to the civil religion can be extremely dangerous. This is especially true in an age when absolutes have disappeared and the dignity of man is itself denigrated. We do, indeed, pay the price for secular dreams.

ELEVEN

THE SECULAR DREAM

"We must consider that we shall be a City Upon a Hill, the eyes of all people upon us," John Winthrop told his Puritan company crossing the Atlantic to find the Massachusetts Bay Colony. The remarkable thing is that four centuries later Americans are still self-consciously trying to build cities on a hill.[1] Winthrop spoke of the city on the hill in terms of Christianity—that is, in terms of traditional religion. Modern Americans in speaking of American society see it in terms of a secular dream. We have, as Harvey Cox notes, become a secular city.[2]

Current and historical analyses of the American dream appear to focus on a number of interdependent themes. I have selected themes which seem to be prevalent in discussions of the American dream as it has become secularized.

Certain contemporary concepts of the American dream have, to a large degree, become banal. The real estate industry, for example, poses it as the buying of a house or condominium somewhere in mundane suburbia. The original principles of rights, resistance, and future optimism have been lost in the mist of secularism.

The American dream has been altered. It has become, in many ways, a matter of pure economics.

Yet, enough of the older memory of what the American dream was meant to be remains with us. In its secular version, the remaining elements of the dream may be expressed in the desire for the absence of governmental restrictions and regulation, the Protestant work ethic, expansionism, and mobility.

ABSENCE OF GOVERNMENTAL RESTRICTION AND REGULATION

A principal theme of the American dream which remains with us is the absence of governmental power and state regulatory authority. James Madison and others observed that the noteworthy accomplishment of the Constitution was that it created the minimum degree of civil government required to maintain order and stability, while preserving maximum individual freedoms. The American was given the broadest scope within which to order his life, organize his agenda, and exercise his rights. As one Norwegian immigrant wrote in a letter home, in America, as in Norway, "there are laws, government, and authorities."[3] But here, he added, "everything is designed to maintain the natural freedom and equality of men."[4]

It was within this "liberated" environment that man was able to pursue his ambitions. The grand expanse of the American frontier gave the visionary room within which to exercise his freedom without infringing on his fellowman. Hence, there was little need for government regulation.

The perception of individual liberty and the American system is critical to the understanding of the American dream. Liberty extended to each man the opportunity to define happiness in his own individual way, and then to pursue it as he so chose. This freedom was, in part, possible in the last century because of the seemingly endless supply of land and natural resources. Liberty, then, meant the right of man to define his goals and purposes—to determine what happiness meant to him—and the right to pursue those goals with singleness of purpose as he would and could. Liberty, so defined, brought a tremendous dynamism to the American community. It would seem to follow that the decline in that liberty through oppressive state regulation has retarded that dynamism and the zealous pursuit of individual goals.

An immigrant's letter written in 1835 illustrates in a simple yet moving manner the value nineteenth-century Americans attached to individual liberty and limited government. The paragraphs reproduced below are preceded by language describing the generosity of Americans and the rights of Americans to vote and stand for public office. This letter illustrates the interdependence, in the minds of many Americans, of liberty and social equality.

Neither in the matter of clothes nor in manners are distinctions noticeable, whether one be a farmer or a clerk. The one enjoys just as much freedom as the other. So long as he comports himself honestly he meets no interference. Everybody is free to travel about the country, wherever he wishes, without passports or papers. Everyone is permitted to engage in whatever business he finds most desirable, in trade or commerce, by land or by water. . . . No duties [taxes] are levied upon goods that are produced in the country and brought to the city by water or by land. In case of death, no registration is required; the survivor, after paying the debts, is free to dispose of the property for himself and his family just as he pleases.[5]

As we have seen, it is arguable that the freedom afforded by the American system is a product of the European Reformation. In fact, just as the Reformation and the emergence of the Calvinist doctrine of predestination freed Protestants from the traditional conduits of grace—the church and the priesthood—so has post-Reformation man been catapulted out of dependence on traditional, political, and social institutions and communities. "He was set free from these limiting and sustaining contexts."[6]

Inasmuch as the American system was the first great "experiment" in Reformation political theory, it is arguable that unparalleled freedom and the absence of stifling governmental regulations were fundamental features of early America. The aim behind the American form of government, writes the late Perry Miller, "was to vindicate the most rigorous ideal of the Reformation."[7] It was within this unrestrained environment that the hard working, risk-taking entrepreneur and adventurer was able to pursue, and often achieve, his highest ideal.

It is noteworthy that post-Reformation liberty was not anarchical; rather, it was disciplined. "God," H. Richard Niebuhr noted, "was the absolute sovereign and his sovereignty exercised the limitation on total individual freedom."[8] This conservatism was, of course, reflected in the philosophy of both the clergy and the framers.

One need not document the study of expansion of the modern state and the spreading of its tentacles into virtually every sphere of human activity. No family, industry, or, indeed, church has escaped the suffocating regulatory power of the civil government.[9] It is revealing that one constant growth area in our society is that portion of government engaged in the promulgation and enforcement of state regulations. The increase in government regulation is, in part, explained by the decrease in cheap land and natural resources. As resources and land have become scarcer, the state has stepped in and "eased" tensions arising from the intensified conflict for limited resources. Nevertheless, increased regulation chills the enterprising and ambitious spirit that has become synonymous with the American dream.

THE MOTIF OF THE RUGGED INDIVIDUAL

Integral to common perceptions of the American dream is that of "individualism."[10] This stemmed in part from Martin Luther's advocation of the "priesthood of the believer." This broke the individual free to intercede with God without the need of an earthly mediator. From this, the "individual" was born. Until that time, individualism as a concept was generally unknown.

Closely related themes include notions of social equality, classlessness, and the right of each American to determine his own agenda. The image of the lone American struggling against hostile elements on the frontier is a persistent motif in popular literature and our national self-perception.[11]

Once again, it is arguable that the "liberation" of the individual from the collective social orders of the medieval era was the product of the Reformation theology. Not only did the theology of John Calvin and Martin Luther free man of the institutional intercessors between God and man, but it also tended to give man an independent identity apart from a social class and the established church. Again man, as an individual, was empowered to approach God independent of his priest. Similarly, the peasantry was no longer seen as a mere extension of the feudal lord. Each and every man was recognized for his inherent worth. These ideas were transported to America and became part of the American dream.

The American Revolution was a seminal event in the rise of nation states, which in turn marked the decline of feudal social models. Freed from the restraints of the feudal order, post-Reformation man was able to leave the land and congregate in urban centers. This independence was illustrative of the emergence of the individual as a separate, social, and political entity. Nowhere was his individualism more celebrated than in America.

Americans tend to see the United States—largely because they think of themselves as individuals evaluated not on the basis of their social background but rather on the basis of their inherent worth—as a land of social equality. Americans often define themselves as a classless society or at least as a nation overwhelmingly dominated by the middle class. One immigrant, for example, observed in a letter to relatives in the Old World: "Here it is not asked, what or who was your father, but the question is, what are you?"[12]

Individualism is an essential feature of the liturgy of the American dream. Each and every American is assigned individual responsibility for his or her own behavior. Like the servants in Christ's parable of the talents, the "success" of each individual is determined by one's enterprising endeavors. The dream perpetuates the belief that any individual in America is afforded the opportunity to transform, through hard work, his or her "talents" into personal and financial gain.

It goes without saying that not even in this limited form has the American dream been open to all Americans. At various periods in history, large sections of American society have been denied access to this part of the American dream. The American Black comes irresistibly to mind as one group dispossessed.[13] Other ethnic and racial groups as well have been systematically excluded. The Irish immigrants in the 1840s and 1850s, for example, were subject to gross and flagrant injustices. Poles and Eastern Europeans in a later period were similarly denied equal footing in the race for the dream.

The revered concept of American individualism has suffered as a result of the growth of the modern state and collective power. The consequences have, in part, contributed to the demise of the American dream (as historically defined). The legalization of abortion illustrates the devaluation of human life and the inherent worth of an individual made in the image of God or as being endowed by the Creator with the absolute right to life. The individual and his rights have ceased to be sacrosanct in modern America. The protection and rights of individuals are increasingly sacrificed in order to pursue the collective rights of various interest groups. The trend, thus, in the courts is to affirm collective rights over individual rights.

Finally, the shift toward collectivism and cradle-to-grave therapeutic state welfare has undermined, if not destroyed, incentive for the exercise of individual responsibility. I have described this elsewhere as "the shift from individual responsibility to a societal responsibility for all acts in American society."[14] "Collectivism, it must be understood, reduces man's individual responsibility and shifts it to the group."[15] Therefore, growth of the paternal welfare state has undermined the spirit of "rugged individualism" and encouraged it to atrophy—resulting in the demise of that quality which gave sustenance to the American dream.

THE PROTESTANT WORK ETHIC

Some notion of the "work ethic" is integral to the definition of the American dream. In his first inaugural address, Richard Nixon—who was later to see his dreams of power crumble by way of exposed corruption—declared that the "American dream does not come to those who fall asleep."[16] In other words, the dream, at least in Nixonian terms, is available only to those willing to work for it. One immigrant in the early nineteenth century captured this truism of the American system:

> There is no one here who snatches it [property] away, like a beast of prey, wanting only to live by the sweat of others and to make himself heir to the money of others. No, everyone must work for his living here, whether he be of low or high estate.[17]

Much has been written about the "work ethic" and what it means in post-Reformation Western society.[18] One commentator has captured the essence of the work ethic in an historic American context, especially as it pertains to the notion of the American dream:

> The Puritan work ethic, now so widely ridiculed, has been a great positive force in American history. Its application meant, for the first time in history, that an individual might by personal effort attain economic security and self-realization. . . . Every Christian was called upon to make the most of his life, not only of his skills and possessions, but to perfect his character as well. This developed the spirit of enterprise and industry which made modern capitalism work. Frugality and strong family life encouraged thrift and

the accumulation of capital. The careful use of time and talent helped form the regular habits and skills upon which the conduct of industry depends. The emphasis on personal responsibility made every individual feel self-important and involved in the total task. The Puritan work ethic enabled the common person to own private property, to have a pride in individual accomplishment, to be important in the life of the entire community, and to have the hope of an unlimited future. The great spaciousness of America—the availability of land and the assurance that as the consequence of hard work, time would bring inevitable success—deeply affected the nation's thinking. For the first time in the history of the world, the emotional impact of such security was available to the common man. He knew the pride and the responsibility of ownership.[19]

From reliance on the Bible—in particular chapter three of the book of Genesis—the Protestant work ethic developed the concept that because of the Fall, man's work is cursed and is therefore made much more difficult. As a consequence, man must be excited to hard work through various incentives. He is not naturally so predisposed to work. The relative freedom of early American society in which one could reap the fruits of one's labor without government regulatory interference or over-taxation was designed to promote such incentives. The steady growth of regulation, however, has resulted in the demise of the work ethic by destroying incentives.

Similarly, decline in traditional religious values has undermined religious concepts of "vocation" and "calling"—such concepts as fostered and promulgated by the likes of John Locke,[20] Benjamin Franklin, and others. The notion that man was called forth to labor for the glory of God is denied in the increasingly secular vision of the work ethic.

Moreover, the earlier extensive reliance on Black slave labor, to a limited extent, debased the relationship between the white man and the fruits of labor. Man, it seemed, could materially gain from the sweat of another man's brow. Of course, slave masters exercised entrepreneurial skills. However, a wholly slaved-based economy undermines the work ethic in its pure sense. Blaine Taylor, knowing the extensive reliance on slave labor in the antebellum South, writes:

This discipline and diligence of the work ethic were lost. Work became simply a way to survive, a way to get money. It lost its inherent value. No longer was it a calling performed for the glory of God.[21]

EXPANSIONISM

The perception of the new world in the formative years of the American dream was that of a land with vast, unchartered expanses of land and a limitless bounty of natural resources. Expansionism—both economic and geographic—was the watchword of the new republic. Indeed, it was the wealth of natural resources and the sweep of the new continent that gave dynamism to the American dream and room for it to flourish.

The geographic frontiers of the new republic were the public face of the American dream—the focus of the future.[22] The frontier was where any man could venture and carve out his piece of the future. Land was cheap, if not free, and there was enough room for all.

Given the scope of the frontier in the early-to-midnineteenth century, one could engage in virtually any activity without being drawn into conflict with one's neighbor. Hence, there was little need for the government to interfere in order to control conflicts. Nineteenth-century man in the American West could fulfill his dream to own real property and to make of it what he was willing to put into it. It was not until the latter half of the nineteenth century, when immigration westward was at its peak, that limits of geographic expansion became apparent. There was the confrontation between the cattle farmers of the West who claimed vast, unfenced tracts of land and the sheepherders who preferred smaller, more defined areas. Both groups resented the farmers who wanted to enclose their small plots with barbed wire. These fences, of course, literally and symbolically limited the mobility of the cattlemen. The resulting confrontations were often bloody and generally went unreported.

The "shrinking" of the American West had its effect on the American dream. The fact that natural resources were apparently limited tarnished the dream and demanded a greater exercise of creativity by those who would pursue it. This may not have been the death knell of the American dream, but it certainly demanded a more creative search for "new frontiers." Fulfillment of the American dream in a world of limited resources requires more than a literal, physical movement westward. To-day the vision demands a creative effort which in turn requires more drive, determination, and imagination. For the modern American inclined toward physical security and comfort, this makes fulfillment of the dream more distant.

Individuals in our society today who are characterized as the epitome of the fulfillment of the American dream tend to be those who have demonstrated this creativity. For example, American astronauts are men and women who have pursued the new frontier of space. They provide the model for the new American dream. That is one reason the NASA-*Challenger* trage-dy in January 1986 so deeply moved the American public. In-cluded among the *Challenger's* crew was a Black, an Oriental, and two women (one of which was a Jew)—all of whom came from rather "simple" backgrounds but aspired to participate in the greatest technological endeavor of all time.

American presidents also are similarly regarded as the per-sonification of the American dream. Thus, we like to extol the lowly backgrounds of our presidents (for example, log-cabin dwellers, a peanut farmer, an orphan, etc.). This confirms our faith that in America anything is possible through hard work.

Similarly, once-poor inventors who came up with a "new" and/or "improved" idea were typically described as the embodi-ment of the American dream. Ray Kroc, the founder of McDon-ald's restaurants, who had the vision for fast-food restaurants, provides a typical example.

Finally, Blaine Taylor has perceptively observed that the abundance of cheap land and natural resources actually contrib-uted to the weakening of certain aspects of the American dream. He writes:

> Ironically, however, in that American push to the West were the seeds that were later to corrupt the Puritan work ethic. The availability of land led to its wasteful use. Its abundance led to speculation and quick profits. The great fortunes which provided the capital for the mechanical age came largely from land speculation, not from hard work.[23]

In sum, the decline of the great and obvious natural re-sources of America does not necessarily mean the dream has ended. Rather, it should encourage creative and resourceful utilization of the natural wealth which remains.

MOBILITY

Mobility is a persistent theme in discussions of the American dream. It has strong roots in the American past in terms of the "right to emigrate."

In its modern use, mobility is used in several different senses. First, the freedom to travel is obviously related to the western migration and the taming of geographic frontiers. Government restrictions on movement and travel would obviously undermine concepts of the American dream.

There is a second sense, however, in which mobility is important to conceptions of the American dream. This sense is related to an earlier millennial vision of America.

As we have seen, there is a determinism which characterizes American perceptions of its role on the world stage. From the days of the Pilgrim Fathers, America has described itself as a "city on a hill"—a new Canaan.[24] Ernest Lee Tuveson notes that from the 1760s onward there emerged "a conception of the colonies as a separate chosen people, destined to complete the Reformation and to inaugurate world recognition."[25]

The Puritans saw themselves as pilgrims and sojourners like Abraham, their destination and citizenship being in the city whose builder and maker is God. Emigration in terms of this faith made them the moving force in the colonies. Not only did the Puritans settle directly in virtually every colony, but many also moved southward in protest against various New England policies which they conceived to be unjust. The faith that made them unyielding in New England made them missionary-minded in their new homes.

The colonists developed an emigrant mentality, as pilgrims, and envisioned America as the promised land. Thus, they looked confidently to the future. It is an interesting and melancholy fact that their descendants—modern Americans—often look nostalgically to the past.

It followed, however, from this perception that since America was called forth to be a great nation, she could not fail. Similarly, her people—a chosen people—had a destiny to fulfill. This destiny was the essence of the American dream. It created a national vision firmly rooted in the belief of its automatic fulfillment of the promised optimistic destiny. This was a form of determinism, but it was a destiny both America and the American could await with confidence.

Therefore, in this second sense "mobility" is the outward demonstration of the national destiny. Indeed, the westward migration of the midnineteenth century, which was the fulfillment of the national heritage, was popularly called "manifest destiny."[26] In other words, mobility became the essence of a grandiose calling for the new nation.

In this respect, manifest destiny is not unlike modern Zionism. The American settler, like the modern Zionist, saw a divine imperative for his migratory behavior. Restraints on the mobility of Americans would be as healthy for the American dream as are Soviet emigration policies for Zionism. The dream suffocates under restraints on free travel.

In a third sense the concept of mobility is essential to the American dream. America is a nation of immigrants. In the nineteenth century the young republic was dependent on the immigrant population for economic and geographic expansion. It was the hope and aspirations of the immigrant which gave the nation its unique dynamism in the late nineteenth century. The new arrivals were the lifeblood of the nation. The constant movement of new Americans was more than symbolic of the continued search for a better life and greater opportunity. Restraints on the mobility of immigrants as they sought to establish themselves in American society and then migrate westward would have been a debilitating blow to the American dream.

The most economically progressive nations of the mid-to-late twentieth century are those which have relied on large immigrant populations. These are the United States, Taiwan, Australia, and, arguably, West Germany and Japan, because of the forced migration and resettlement policies following World War II. This is explained, in part at least, because the builders of these nations arrived by choice, and they came to work and to achieve a lifestyle better than that they left behind. The strength of the American dream is not that it is coerced upon anyone, but that it is a vision voluntarily pursued.

THE DARKER SIDE
No treatment of the secular vision of the American dream would be complete without acknowledging its darker side.

Cutthroat competition and pursuit of the material offerings of the American system destroy many along the way. The weak are dispossessed or often ignored or left without recourse in the stampede for material rewards.

There are ethnic and racial groups who have been systematically excluded from participating fairly in the quest for the dream. Unfortunately, there is little or no incentive to recognize or assist those lacking the faculties to compete equally within the system.

Finally, the dream has often degenerated into crass materialism and an orgy of self-indulgence. Moreover, success and achievement within the system are typically defined in material terms. Rarely are nontangible or spiritual factors recognized as fulfillment of the dream. Ironically, the divorce of spiritual fulfillment from material success devalues the meaning and substance of the fruits of the American dream.

It has become fashionable to conduct postmortems on the American dream. The dream for many has become a nightmare—a legacy perpetuating injustices rather than promoting equality. The strong and the rich, it is said, are getting stronger and richer, while the weak and poor are getting weaker and poorer. Shrinking natural resources and available land have had a further psychological effect on the inherent optimism of the dream entirely. The environment and society which gave rise to public perceptions of the American dream have unquestionably been dealt a debilitating blow. The question remains, does the sense of that dream survive?

The pillars of traditional conceptions of the American dream are being subtly undermined. Pessimism entered with the breakdown along with self-regulating liberal concepts of the state and society. Virtually all aspects of human activity, including free enterprise, have been constrained by state regulation. We have also witnessed a devaluation in the worth of the individual.

Fulfillment of the American dream requires a much different course today than it did a century ago. No longer is mere physical westward migration and the acquisition of cheap land (property) the essence of the secular dream. The obvious aspects of nineteenth-century aspirations cease to be as attractive or possible to twentieth-century Americans. Fulfillment of the dream today demands a more creative approach to wealth, cre-

ation, avoidance of state regulation, efficient use of limited resources, and entrepreneurial skills.

In the end it will also mean salvaging the soul of America.
Religion is the lifeblood which fuels the heart, and without it the
heart stops beating.

PART FOUR

COMING HOME

Religion is as central to a culture's self-definition as speech or tool-making. It is the key to culture. Every nation finds its legitimacy in being a part of a larger context. The cosmos, the movement of history, or the purpose of God provides a nation with its reason for being. Society is never merely a social contract, an association of individuals who band together out of mutual self-interest. It always transcends the social and finds its meaning in the sacred.

Robert Bellah (1976)

TWELVE

ADAM REDUX

A century ago, the image that embodied the American ideal was a figure of heroic innocence and vast potentialities, poised at the start of a new history. It was not surprising, in a Bible-reading generation, that the new man was most easily identified with Adam before the Fall. Adam was the first, the archetypal man. Thus, there was, as R. W. B. Lewis writes, the birth of the "American Adam."[1]

With the advent of the twentieth century, the innocence of earlier generations has faded. It has, unfortunately, been replaced by the tarnished view of life and people as provided for by the American secular society.

Christopher Lasch in *The Culture of Narcissism* cuts to the quick with a penetrating analysis of the loss of American innocence and the decay of American culture.[2] Evidence abounds of the alienation, loneliness, and despair that characterize modern America.[3]

At issue is what future man and his society will look like and be like. Involved in the struggle for tomorrow will be the proponents of the secular age and those who affirm the continued relevance of traditional religion. The outcome of this struggle will certainly be reflected at the polls and in decisions of government and the courts. However, it will be settled first of all in the religious decisions of men. Inescapably, history is the outworking of religious commitments.

Hope for the future will hinge on how dedicated contemporary Americans are to recovering at least some of the ideals fostered by the American dream. It will mean asserting the rights of people and, when rights are violated, resistance to the infringing authority.

THE RIGHTS OF PEOPLE

The rights of *all* people must be respected and protected. But why?

The Declaration of Independence places the concept of rights on a religious foundation. It establishes them in terms of man's relationship to the Creator—"all men are *created* equal [and] are endowed by their *Creator* with certain unalienable rights."

The older biblical theism taught the *createdness* that is reflected in the Declaration. This theism teaches that all people are *created* in the image of God. Being created in God's image carries with it many facets. The conception of man made in the image of God can be summarized by saying that man, like God, has personhood, a measure of self-transcendence, intelligence, morality, love, and creativity.

Being created in God's image meant, to those who came before us, that man was to manifest the Creator because man acquired in a reflected manner the characteristics of God. This, on account of his createdness, afforded man great dignity and worth. "It also meant man, instead of being a one-dimensional machine-entity, was a three-dimensional human-entity."[4]

The decline in the worth and dignity of people is the major dilemma of the modern world. The wholesale torturing and imprisoning of entire populations is a recurring tragedy of the twentieth century. Terrorism and the "blowing away" of people is an almost daily drama. Moreover, the entire Western culture systematically degrades human existence by viewing people as consumers to be manipulated. And with the rise of abortion, infanticide, and euthanasia, we are near the ultimate plateau of the degradation of the human race. As a consequence, a principal task of this generation is in keeping *humanness* in the human race. This will, in turn, require retrieving the soul of America.

Recovering the religious soul will be very difficult. "God, one of the most important political figures in Western history, is dying," writes Michael Harrington.[5]

This is true even within Christianity itself. Modern Christianity, through television and radio, has spoken its message to more people more times and more ways than ever before in history. However, as George Gallup, Jr., writes: "When we begin to probe just how important religion is in the individual lives of various people, there sometimes appears to be a lack of substance behind the basic belief in God."[6] Gallup continues:

> [A]s a people, we lack deep levels of individual spiritual commitment. One sign of this is that the level of ethics in this country seems to be declining—at least in terms of public perceptions of ethical behavior. . . . [W]e found there's very little difference between the churched and the un-churched in terms of their general view on ethical matters, and also their practical ethical responses in various situations.[7]

A spiritual superficiality marks much of modern religion. It lacks the substance that the earlier versions of American Christianity possessed and, as a consequence, does not significantly affect the American mind. This is unfortunate since Americans, as do other people of the world, face a nihilistic secularism that threatens to reduce humanity to cogs within the machine.

Michael Harrington, himself an atheist, writes: "I think that in the late twentieth century serious atheists and serious believers have more in common with one another than with mindless, *de facto* atheists (who often affirm some vague and sentimental God) and routine churchgoers":

> Both have looked into the same void at the center of this incredible age. . . . [T]he committed believers and unbelievers now have the same enemy: the humdrum nihilism of every-day life in much of Western society.[8]

The "humdrum nihilism of everyday life" has virtually sapped any sense of true happiness from throngs of contemporary people. Modern man, with his sense of despair, sees little light at the end of the tunnel.

Traditional religion provides little solace for the modern malaise. Contemporary Christianity is more waving of arms and contentless sermons and "Christian" writings than thinking. It has gone "mindless."

Such an indictment does not apply to all Christians, of course. There are many Christians who give sacrificially of their time and resources to try to transform the spiritual/moral squalor now present in America. I personally know of several individuals and organizations acting aggressively to save the lives of unborn children, care for the needs of the handicapped and the elderly, rescue those oppressed for their faith, and confront other vital concerns. Such Christians are performing a necessary and loving service, and I do not mean to slight their sacrifice and commitment.

Their number, however, is almost negligible when compared with the overwhelming majority of people who profess to be Christians yet remain unmoved by the great suffering around them, choosing instead to indulge their own comforts. Tragically, I believe this majority includes many who are viewed as Christian "leaders."

Current ministers and Christian personalities are, by and large, mere shadows of the great Christian leaders of the past. "They certainly do not compare favorably," writes New York University professor Neil Postman, "with well-known evangelicals of an earlier period, such as Jonathan Edwards, George Whitefield and Charles Finney, who were men of great learning, theological subtlety and powerful expositional skills."[9]

Unfortunately, much of this has to do with "television Christianity" which, in my opinion, is one of the sad commentaries on the modern Christian church. With much of it characterized by hucksterism and shallowness, it is little wonder that not only the average Christian but Christian leaders as well are ineffective as they meet face-to-face with secular culture.

Of course, the return of the educated clergy would be important. However, since seminary education appears to be severely deficient in a study of the humanities—and since a growing number of seminaries have succumbed to theological liberalism—such is only a faint hope.

One point is evident. Without a clear religious base for the advocation of rights, freedom, and liberty, the American culture hangs on a slender thread much like Jonathan Edwards's sinner dangling over the fiery furnaces of hell.

RESISTANCE
Recovery of the concept of resistance—not revolution—against the tyranny of governmental authority is essential in our times. The American dream instructs that the people can so resist. Indeed, as Jefferson wrote, "it is their right, it is their duty, to throw off [tyrannous] government."

This fact is important not only for America but even more so for the oppressed persons around the world, especially in view of the steady decline of free states and the rise of authoritarianism.

The growth and power of the state is the most significant political development of the twentieth century.[10] By 1950, what has commonly been called the "free world" had shrunk from over 90 to less than 70 percent of the world's population. By 1980, the number of Communist regimes had reached twenty-five, almost twice the total that existed in 1950. Before the year 2000—if current trends continue—the ratio between free and Communist states may well shrink from a ratio of 65:35 to 50:50. The implications from such a shift are enormous.[11]

If Americans totally lose sight of the resistance principle, we have nothing to say to dissidents who find themselves in the Gulag for merely speaking their mind. In this crucial area, America can be the hope for an oppressed world. If we are shouting anything from the housetops, it should be: "Resist the tyrant."

This is where one large section of Christianity, and their professed intellectuals, are overtly naive. Over two centuries after the fact, it is still being debated whether or not Christians should have supported the American Revolution.[12] It is painfully odd that a religion that has since the time of Christ advocated freedom and liberty should advocate a pacificism that will inexorably lead to oppressed classes of people.

Chapter 13 of the Book of Romans is the standard text used to urge what Jefferson referred to in the Declaration as the predisposition of people "to suffer, while evils are sufferable, than to right themselves by abolishing the forms to which they are accustomed."

I have discussed the grounds for resistance in detail elsewhere.[13] Let us focus, however, on the one verse commonly used to encourage simplistic obedience to oppressive governmental acts—Romans 13:1. It reads: "Let every soul be subject unto the higher powers. For there is no power but of God: the powers that be are ordained of God."

The Reformation thinkers, the early American clergy, and writers such as John Locke and others interpreted this passage as permitting what they termed "the constitutional theory [of resistance] allowing for opposition [to governmental authority] by 'inferior magistrates.' "[14] This was advocated in a number of leading works written soon after the Reformation which were later influential on American thinking. Especially important was the *Vindiciae contra Tyrannos*[15] as discussed in chapter five.

The constitutional theory of resistance argues that the higher powers ordained by God include at least two agencies, both representatives of the people, who may lawfully resist government authority in certain circumstances. One such agency was said to be popularly elected national officials.[16] In American government, if the president were, for example, to declare himself a dictator, Congress could resist him on the grounds that it too, being a body that represents the people, is ordained of God.

A second class would include local community leaders. These local officers, again, as representatives of the people, could resist higher government gone bad. They are also ordained of God.

If chapter 13 of Romans is not read at least in this fashion, a people could not resist the likes of a Stalin or a Hitler. Surely God does not ordain murderers to rob, pillage, and oppress the people. Such simplistic readings of biblical texts would lead to tyranny in the name of God.

Some Christians tend to forget that Israel had its beginnings in resistance. Moses was a resistance leader when he led the Exodus. In fact, as Michael Walzer writes in *Exodus and Revolution:* "Moses' importance is not personal but political—as leader of the people or mediator between the people and God—for this is a *political* history: it is about slavery and freedom, law and rebellion."[17]

Surely, we cannot condemn Martin Luther King, Jr., who, in the fashion of Moses, led the civil rights movement on behalf of the Blacks of America. Not only was he squarely rooted in Christian teachings when he stood against government authorities who oppressed Blacks, but also consistent with centuries of teachings that stand for resistance in the face of tyranny.

This is the American dream. One hopes it can become a dream in Communist and other totalitarian countries. Then the freedom that yet reigns in America can find roots in soil that cries to us for help.

TOWARD THE FUTURE

There are no golden ages. Greece was not a golden age, nor was there one when the Roman Empire established its *Pax Romana.* The same can be said of early America, even though it gave birth to the dream that has been the focus of this book. We can, however, look to a past in America where "freedom" was more free and men dreamed of a future where life, liberty, and the pursuit of happiness would be assured.

The present age runs on the twin rails of apathy and despair. As the twentieth century nears its end, the conviction grows that many other things are ending too. As Christopher Lasch notes: "Storm warnings, portents, hints of catastrophe haunt our times. The 'sense of an ending,' which has given shape to so much of twentieth-century literature, now pervades the popular imagination as well":

> The Nazi holocaust, the threat of nuclear annihilation, the depletion of natural resources, well-founded predictions of ecological disaster have fulfilled the poetic prophecy, giving concrete historical substance to the nightmare, or death wish, that avant-garde artists were first to express. The question of whether the world will end in fire or in ice, with a bang or a whimper, no longer interests artists alone. Impending disaster has become an everyday concern, so commonplace and familiar that nobody any longer gives much thought to how disaster might be averted.[18]

As a consequence, people "busy themselves instead with survival strategies, measures designed to prolong their own lives, or programs guaranteed to ensure good health and peace of mind."[19]

Amidst the rat race of existence, peace of mind has become a major goal of countless modern Americans. The search for peace has too often led to drugs, music, entertainment, and other numbing processes which allow many people to survive modern life.

Too often religion, including Christianity, becomes a numbing effect and a form of escapism. This is evident in the distortions of Christianity which promote mindless experience, without knowledge. Moreover, escapism, often called "entertainment," is the vogue. People retreat into their "comfortable" church services, their "comfortable" fellowships, and their "comfortable" five-minute "devotions," presuming they must shield themselves from the decaying world "out there" when what they should be doing is influencing it.

Ending—that is the theme that lays a dark shadow over America as we near the final years of the twentieth century. The proliferation of such phenomena as abortion and homosexuality signal an end to the birth process. The future, of course, is in children. Pornography, immediate sexual gratification without having children, underlies the end of the birth process.

The sense of ending is reflected in a birthrate which has fallen below the replacement level. Were it not for immigration, this low level of reproduction would cause the United States' population to begin shrinking before the next century.[20] It takes an average of 2.2 births per woman to maintain population at a steady level. Because the trend in America is following European patterns, "some demographers say there is reason to believe the U.S. rate could fall to 1.6."[21]

Because people are having fewer children, this means that the American population is growing progressively older. In fact, if the current trend continues, sometime in the early twenty-first century one-third of the American population will be sixty-five or older.[22]

Aged nations, wedded to their own comfort and fearful of change, tend to commit suicide. This may be particularly true of the entire Caucasian elite of the West. "Such has been the fate of practically every elite [group] that has ever existed; as its demands upon the environment have mounted, its viability has been threatened until it has been swept aside by tougher and more dynamic people," writes Germaine Greer.[23]

Such "gerontacracies" invariably take steps to preserve their supremacy. They become more authoritarian, secretive, and militaristic. This is tellingly illustrated by the aged leadership of both the United States and the Soviet Union. We must not forget that it is the young who fight and die in wars.

However, as it becomes readily apparent that the aged are a "burden," we must be concerned with how modern secularistic society will react. Will a society which has assumed the right to kill infants (through abortion and infanticide) also assume the right to kill older adults who are judged a social nuisance? If one is predisposed to consider forced killing of the aged (euthanasia) as a foolish assumption, we must remember the malleability of modern American society.

The ending syndrome also brings to mind the surge in teenage suicide, which is now the second leading cause of death of persons aged fifteen to twenty-four. The modern secular "paradise" has a lot of people wanting to exit it and fast.

Dr. Shervert Frazier, director of the National Institute of Mental Health and chairman of the Task Force on Youth Suicide, has noted that among the factors responsible for the burgeoning teenage suicide rate are changes in family structure and the *declining influence of religion* in America. He said:

> [Religion] is a built-in future concept. A belief system was what tided a lot of us over as adolescents. We had a belief in the future, that there was somebody up there watching out for me and taking care of me.[24]

Dr. Frazier notes that true religion has that built-in future concept which includes the compassionate belief that there is a loving God who cares for people. That, he says, has been lost. Maybe "given away" is a better phrase. Too many Christians have simply "declined" to influence the culture. As a result, many people, especially the young, have lost hope and see no future.

Obviously, the consensus of the American people must change if there is to be any hope for a future orientation. This means that the focus of Christianity must shift to a compassionate mode in terms of helping people cope with the complexity of contemporary life. This would mean effective social action.

I personally do not see this in the immediate future. It would take a complete revamping of the mentality of contemporary Christianity. It would mean a movement away from self-indulgent construction projects, "Christian" knickknacks, and other trivialities. It would mean channeling money and other resources to meet the real needs of people. Unfortunately, many Christian leaders, caught within the confines of materialism, will have a difficult time moving in other directions. It seems to be a paradox, but Christ noted that one serves either materialism *or* God. One cannot serve both.

One thing is certain. Without an optimistic—but realistic—striving toward building a future, America will face hard times. That sense of ending may become a reality.

NO NIGHTMARE

"Redux" is defined as returning to a healthy state. For America to return to a healthy state, she must regain her soul. It is as if America has sold her soul for a bowl of pottage.

The confidence of the American people has been shaken. The American Adam, who could—if only in mind—overcome all obstacles, needs to make an encore. I am *not* here speaking of anything but the need for strength and stamina in the face of impending crises. This will require Americans pulling together, even if it means, as Michael Harrington urges, atheists, agnostics, and believers pulling together. Certainly, we of the present owe it to our posterity to do all we can to see that freedom prevails.

The American dream has carried many a long way. It has not been without its problems. But there is no reason the dream should become a holocaustic nightmare.

NOTES

CHAPTER ONE: THE "ACCIDENT"

1. Paul Simon, "American Tune," *Here Comes Rhymin' Simon* (New York: Columbia Records, 1973).
2. Jean-François Revel, *How Democracies Perish* (Garden City, N.Y.: Doubleday, 1983), p. 3.
3. *Ibid.*, pp. 3-4.
4. Harvey Cox, *The Seduction of the Spirit* (New York: Simon and Schuster, 1973), p. 121.
5. Gilbert K. Chesterton, *What I Saw in America* (New York: Dodd, Mead, 1922), pp. 11-12, 7.

CHAPTER TWO: THE AMERICAN MIND

1. John Adams, *Papers of John Adams*, Robert J. Taylor, ed., Vol. IV (Cambridge: Belknap Press, 1979), p. 195.
2. John Adams, *Works*, Vol. I (Boston: Little, Brown, 1856), p. 232.
3. Thomas Jefferson, *Jefferson Himself*, Bernard Mayo, ed. (Boston: Houghton Mifflin, 1942), p. 70.
4. *Ibid.* (emphasis supplied).
5. A parchment copy of the Declaration of Independence is found in Carl L. Becker, *The Declaration of Independence: A Study in the History of Political Ideas* (1922) (New York: Vintage Books, 1958), pp. 187-193.
6. Henry Grunwald, "The Morning After the Fourth: Have We Kept Our Promise?" *Time* (July 14, 1975), p. 19.
7. Bill Moyers, "Prudence Reigns," *Newsweek* (July 28, 1975), p. 72.
8. Alexis de Tocqueville, *Democracy in America*, Vol. 1 (New York: Vintage Books, 1954), p. 26.
9. As quoted by Jack P. Greene and William G. McLaughlin, *Preachers and Politicians: Two Essays on the Origin of the American Revolution* (Worchester: American Antiquarian Society, 1977), p. 48.
10. Robert E. Brown, *Middle-Class Democracy and the Revolution in Massachusetts, 1691-1780* (Ithaca: Cornell University Press, 1955), p. 401.

11. Daniel J. Boorstin, *The Genius of American Politics* (Chicago: University of Chicago Press, 1955), p. 68.
12. Peter F. Drucker, *The Future of Industrial Man* (New York: John Day, 1942), p. 219.
13. *Ibid.*, p. 222.
14. *Ibid.*, p. 224.
15. *Ibid.*, p. 219.
16. *See generally* Friedrich Gentz, "The French and American Revolutions Compared," *Three Revolutions*, S. T. Possony, ed. and John Quincy Adams, trans. (Chicago: Regnery, 1959).
17. Clinton Rossiter, *Seedtime of the Republic: The Origin of the American Tradition of Political Liberty* (New York: Harcourt, Brace, 1953), p. 119.
18. Benjamin Franklin, *The Papers of Benjamin Franklin,* Vol. I (New Haven: Yale University Press, 1959), p. 62 (emphasis in original).
19. Henry Steele Commager, *Jefferson, Nationalism, and the Enlightenment* (New York: George Braziller, 1975), p. 85 (emphasis in original).
20. James Burnham, *Congress and the American Tradition* (Chicago: Regnery, 1959), p. 24.
21. *See generally* Samuel Rutherford, *Lex Rex; or, the Law and the Prince* (1644) (Harrisonburg, Va.: Sprinkle Publications, 1980).
22. *See, for example,* Mark A. Noll, Nathan O. Hatch, and George M. Marsden, *The Search for Christian America* (Westchester, Ill.: Crossway Books, 1983), pp. 88-91.
23. As quoted by John Chester Miller, *The Wolf by the Ears: Thomas Jefferson and Slavery* (New York: Free Press, 1977), p. 8.
24. *See* Becker, *op. cit.,* pp. 213-217.
25. *See, for example,* Noll, Hatch and Marsden, *op. cit.*

CHAPTER THREE: THE CLERGY

1. *See generally* Harry S. Stout, *The New England Soul: Preaching and Religious Culture in Colonial New England* (New York: Oxford University Press, 1986).
2. Alice M. Baldwin, *The New England Clergy and the American Revolution* (New York: Frederick Ungar, 1928), p. 3.
3. Mark A. Noll, *Christians in the American Revolution* (Washington, D.C.: Christian University Press, 1977), p. 30.
4. Baldwin, *op. cit.,* p. xii.
5. *Ibid.,* p. 3. *See also* Stout, *op. cit.,* p. 5.
6. *Ibid.*
7. *Ibid.* Many of the Baptists and separate Congregational clergy were not educated men. In 1764 there were but two liberally educated Baptist ministers in New England. Before 1783, there were a good many more, however. *Ibid.*
8. *Ibid.,* p. 4.
9. Stout, *op. cit.,* p. 3.
10. Baldwin, *op. cit.,* p. 4.
11. Kenneth L. Woodward, "When God Had No Competition: New In-

sights into the Puritans' Pulpit Culture," *Newsweek* (October 20, 1986), p. 73.

12. Baldwin, *op. cit.*, pp. 5-6.
13. *Ibid.*, p. 6.
14. Stout, *op. cit.*, pp. 3-4 (emphasis supplied).
15. *Ibid.*, p. 4.
16. *Ibid.*, pp. 4-5 (emphasis in original).
17. Jonathan Mayhew, *A Defense of the Observation on the Charter and Conduct of the Society for the Propagation of the Gospel in Foreign Parts* (Boston, 1763), p. 39.
18. Baldwin, *op. cit.*, p. 7.
19. Stout, *op. cit.*, p. 6.
20. See, for example, John Dunn, *The Political Thought of John Locke: An Historical Account of the Argument of the 'Two Treatises of Government'* (Cambridge: Cambridge University Press, 1969), pp. 7-8; John Dunn, "The Politics of Locke in England and America in the Eighteenth Century," *John Locke: Problems and Perspectives*, John W. Yolton, ed. (Cambridge: Cambridge University Press, 1969), pp. 45-80.
21. Baldwin, *op. cit.*, pp. 7-8.
22. *Ibid.*, p. 8.
23. *Ibid.*, p. 10.
24. *Ibid.*, pp. 10-11.
25. *Ibid.*, p. 12.
26. *Ibid.*
27. Stout, *op. cit.*, p. 7.

CHAPTER FOUR: LOCKE

1. Donald S. Lutz, *The Relative Influence of European Writers on Late Eighteenth-Century American Political Thought*, American Political Science Review, Vol. 78 (1984), p. 192.
2. Mark A. Noll, Nathan O. Hatch, and George M. Marsden, *The Search for Christian America* (Westchester, Ill.: Crossway Books, 1983), p. 29.
3. *Ibid.*
4. Clinton Rossiter, *Seedtime of the Republic: The Origin of the American Tradition of Political Liberty* (New York: Harcourt, Brace, 1953), p. 135.
5. *Ibid.*
6. Harry S. Stout, *The New England Soul: Preaching and Religious Culture in Colonial New England* (New York: Oxford University Press, 1986), p. 8.
7. Sydney E. Ahlstrom, *A Religious History of the American People* (New Haven: Yale University Press, 1972), p. 1090 (emphasis in original).
8. Rossiter, *op. cit.*, p. 53.
9. *Ibid.*
10. *See generally* Perry Miller, *The New England Mind* (New York: Macmillan, 1939); Perry Miller and T. H. Johnson, *The Puritans* (New York: American Book Company, 1938).
11. Rossiter, *op. cit.*, p. 53.

178 □ AN AMERICAN DREAM

12. Stout, *op. cit.*, p. 7.
13. *Ibid.*
14. Rossiter, *op. cit.*, p. 53.
15. *Ibid.*, p. 54.
16. *Ibid.*
17. Roscoe Pound, "Common Law," *Encyclopedia of the Social Sciences*, Vol. IV (New York: Macmillan, 1937), p. 55.
18. Rossiter, *op. cit.*, p. 54.
19. *Ibid.*, pp. 54-55.
20. *Ibid.*, p. 55.
21. *Ibid.*, p. 120.
22. *Ibid.*
23. *Ibid.*, p. 55 (emphasis in original).
24. *Ibid.*
25. John Dunn, *The Political Thought of John Locke: An Historical Account of the Argument of the 'Two Treatises of Government'* (Cambridge: Cambridge University Press, 1969), p. 256.
26. *Ibid.*, p. 259 (emphasis in original).
27. *See generally* C. Gregg Singer, *From Rationalism to Irrationality: The Decline of the Western Mind from the Renaissance to the Present* (Philipsburg, N.J.: Presbyterian and Reformed, 1979).
28. Edward S. Corwin, *The "Higher Law" Background of American Constitutional Law* (Ithaca, N.Y.: Cornell University Press, 1955), p. 61.
29. *See generally* Lutz, *op. cit.*
30. *See generally* John Locke, *Two Treatises of Civil Government* (1690) (New York: Cambridge University Press, 1970).
31. *See generally* Sterling Power Lamprecht, *The Moral and Political Philosophy of John Locke* (1918) (New York: Russell and Russell, 1962); Richard I. Aaron, *John Locke* (1937), 2nd ed. (Oxford: Clarendon Press, 1955).
32. Corwin, *op. cit.*, p. 63.
33. *Ibid.*, p. 64.
34. *Ibid.*, p. 63.
35. *Ibid.*, pp. 63-64.
36. As quoted by Sanford Levinson, *"The Constitution"* in American Civil Religion, The Supreme Court Review (1979), p. 128.
37. Rossiter, *op. cit.*, p. 40.
38. Corwin, *op. cit.*, p. 67.
39. *Ibid.*, p. 69.

CHAPTER FIVE: THE GROUNDS FOR REVOLUTION

1. Herbert D. Foster, *International Calvinism Through Locke and the Revolution of 1688*, American Historical Review, Vol. 32, p. 475 (1927).
2. *Ibid.*
3. *Ibid.*
4. Michael Walzer, *The Revolution of the Saints: A Study in the Origin of Radical Politics* (Cambridge: Harvard University Press, 1965), p. viii.
5. Foster, *op. cit.*, p. 476.

6. *Ibid.*, p. 487.
7. *Ibid.*
8. *Ibid.*
9. *Ibid.*
10. *Ibid.*, p. 488.
11. *Ibid.*
12. *Ibid.*
13. *Ibid.*, p. 489.
14. *Ibid.*
15. *Ibid.*, p. 490.
16. *Ibid.*
17. *Ibid.*, p. 491.
18. *Ibid.*
19. *Ibid.*
20. *Ibid.*
21. *Ibid.*
22. *Ibid.*, p. 492.
23. *Ibid.*
24. *Ibid.*, p. 493.
25. *Ibid.*, p. 494.
26. *Ibid.*
27. *Ibid.*, p. 495.
28. *Ibid.*, pp. 495-496.
29. *See generally* John Calvin, *Institutes of the Christian Religion* (1536) (Grand Rapids, Mich.: Eerdmans, 1953).
30. Foster, *op. cit.*, p. 496.
31. *Ibid.*
32. *Ibid.*, p. 497.
33. *Ibid.*, pp. 497-498.
34. The complete title page reads: *Vindiciae contra Tyrannos, sive de principis in populum, populique in principem legitima potestate,* Stephano Iunio Bruto Celta, auctore, Basle, 1579. The first edition, in Latin, was published in Switzerland under a false Edinburgh imprint. A French translation appeared in 1581 and an English translation in 1648, under the title *A Defense of Liberty Against Tyrants.*
35. Peter Laslett, "Introduction" to John Locke, *Two Treatises of Civil Government* (Cambridge: Cambridge University Press, 1960), pp. 131-135. *Also see* Carl L. Becker, *The Declaration of Independence: A Study in the History of Political Ideas* (New York: Vintage Books, 1958), pp. 33-34.
36. George H. Sabine and Thomas L. Thorson, *A History of Political Theory,* 4th ed. (Hinsdale, Ill.: Dryden Press, 1973), p. 348.
37. *See generally* Quentin Skinner, *The Foundations of Modern Political Thought,* Vol. 2 (Cambridge: Cambridge University Press, 1978).
38. This fact as well as an analysis of the *Vindiciae contra Tyrannos* is presented in Daniel L. Dreisbach, *Late Reformation Resistance Theology and Its Revival in Current American Politics,* a paper presented to the Symposium on American Politics, Social Studies Centre, Oxford University on February 23, 1983.

39. Sabine and Thorson, *op. cit.*, p. 352.
40. Skinner, *op. cit.*, p. 305.
41. Harold J. Laski, "Historical Introduction," in Junius Brutus, *A Defence Of Liberty Against Tyrants: A Translation of the Vindiciae contra Tyrannos* (London: G. Bell and Sons, 1924), pp. 57-59.
42. *Ibid.*, p. 54.
43. Rev. J. Neville Figgis, "Political Thought in the Sixteenth Century," *The Cambridge Modern History: The Wars of Religion*, Vol. III, Chap. XII (New York: Macmillan, 1934), p. 1164.
44. Gerald Runkle, *A History of Western Political Theory* (New York: Ronald Press, 1968), p. 211.
45. *See generally* Dreisbach, *op. cit.*
46. Laski, *op. cit.*, p. 42.
47. *Ibid.*, p. 42.
48. Dreisbach, *op. cit.*, p. 8.
49. Laski, *op. cit.*, p. 48.
50. *Ibid.*, p. 41.
51. Skinner, *op. cit.*, p. 327.
52. *Ibid.*, p. 320.
53. *Cambridge Modern History,* Vol. III, *op. cit.*, p. 763.
54. Laski, *op. cit.*, p. 53.
55. *Cambridge Modern History,* Vol. III, *op. cit.*, p. 764.
56. *Ibid.*, p. 768.
57. Skinner, *op. cit.*, p. 332.
58. *Ibid.*, p. 336.
59. *Ibid.*, p. 315.
60. *Ibid.*, p. 317.
61. *See generally* Dreisbach, *op. cit.*
62. *Cambridge Modern History,* Vol. III, *op. cit.*, p. 761.
63. William Archibald Dunning, *A History of Political Theories: From Luther to Montesquieu* (New York: Macmillan, 1920), p. 38.
64. *Ibid.*, p. 49.
65. *Ibid.*, pp. 49-50.
66. Sabine and Thorson, *op. cit.*, p. 353.
67. Skinner, *op. cit.*, p. 332.
68. Dunning, *op. cit.*, p. 54.
69. *Ibid.*, p. 52.
70. *Ibid.*, p. 53.
71. Laski, *op. cit.*, p. 44.
72. Foster, *op. cit.*, p. 485.
73. *Ibid.*, p. 498.
74. *Ibid.*, p. 499.

CHAPTER SIX: THE GOOD OF THE PEOPLE

1. Stuart M. Robinson, *"And . . . we mutually pledge . . ."* (New Canaan, Conn.: The Long House, 1964), p. 7.
2. Harry S. Stout, *The New England Soul: Preaching and Religious Culture in Colonial New England* (New York: Oxford University Press, 1986), p. 9.

3. Mark A. Noll, Nathan O. Hatch, and George M. Marsden, *The Search for Christian America* (Westchester, Ill.: Crossway Books, 1983), p. 29.
4. Robinson, *op. cit.*, p. 35.
5. Alice M. Baldwin, *The New England Clergy and the American Revolution* (New York: Frederick Ungar, 1928), pp. 13, 14.
6. *Ibid.*, p. 14.
7. *Ibid.*, p. 15.
8. *Ibid.*
9. *Ibid.*
10. *Ibid.*, p. 16.
11. *Ibid.*
12. *Ibid.*, p. 17.
13. *Ibid.*, p. 18.
14. *Ibid.*, p. 19.
15. *Ibid.*, p. 22.
16. *Ibid.*, p. 23.
17. *Ibid.*
18. *Ibid.*
19. *Ibid.*, p. 24.
20. *Ibid.*, p. 27.
21. *Ibid.*, p. 29.
22. *Ibid.*
23. *Ibid.*, p. 31.
24. *Ibid.*, p. 32.
25. *Ibid.*
26. *Ibid.*
27. *Ibid.*, p. 34.
28. *Ibid.*, p. 34.
29. *Ibid.*, p. 35.
30. *Ibid.*
31. *Ibid.*, pp. 35-36.
32. *Ibid.*, p. 37.
33. *Ibid.*, p. 38.
34. *Ibid.*, p. 38-39.
35. *Ibid.*, p. 39.
36. *Ibid.*, p. 40.
37. *Ibid.*, pp. 42-43.
38. *Ibid.*, p. 45.
39. *Ibid.*

CHAPTER SEVEN: THE REVOLT OF THE BLACK REGIMENT

1. *See generally* Alan Heimert and Perry Miller, eds., *The Great Awakening* (Indianapolis: Bobbs-Merrill, 1967). *Also see* Harry S. Stout, *The New England Soul: Preaching and Religious Culture in Colonial New England* (New York: Oxford University Press, 1986), pp. 185-211.
2. Alice M. Baldwin, *The New England Clergy and the American Revolution* (New York: Frederick Ungar, 1928), p. 58.
3. *Ibid.*

4. Mark A. Noll, Nathan O. Hatch, and George Marsden, *The Search for Christian America* (Westchester, Ill.: Crossway Books, 1983), p. 54.
5. *Ibid.*
6. *See generally* Carl Bridenbaugh, *Mitre and Sceptre: Transatlantic Faiths, Ideas, Personalities, and Politics* (London: Oxford University Press, 1962).
7. John Adams, *Works,* Vol. X (New York: AMS Press, 1971), p. 185.
8. Noll, Hatch and Marsden, *op. cit.*, p. 55.
9. *Ibid.*
10. *Ibid.*
11. Clinton Rossiter, *Seedtime of the Republic: The Origin of the American Tradition of Political Liberty* (New York: Harcourt, Brace, 1953), p. 56.
12. *Ibid.*, p. 57.
13. *Ibid.*
14. *Ibid.*
15. *Ibid.*
16. *Ibid.*
17. *Ibid.*, p. 58.
18. Baldwin, *op. cit.*, p. 66.
19. *Ibid.*, pp. 67-68.
20. *Ibid.*, p. 68.
21. *Ibid.*, p. 83.
22. *Ibid.*, p. 98.
23. *Ibid.*, p. 106.
24. *Ibid.*, p. 111.
25. *Ibid.*
26. *Ibid.*, p. 112.
27. *Ibid.*, p. 113.
28. *Ibid.*
29. *Ibid.*, p. 118.
30. *Ibid.*, p. 119.
31. *Ibid.*, p. 122.
32. *Ibid.*, p. 123.
33. *Ibid.*
34. *Ibid.*
35. *Ibid.*, p. 125. *See generally* Stout, *op. cit.*
36. *Ibid.*, p. 126.
37. *Ibid.*, p. 130.
38. *See generally* Stout, *op. cit.*
39. Samuel West, *A Sermon Preached Before the Honorable Council and the Honorable House of Representatives of the Colony of Massachusetts Bay* (Boston, 1776), pp. 20-21 (emphasis supplied).
40. Stewart M. Robinson, *"And . . . we mutually pledge . . ."* (New Canaan, Conn.: The Long House, 1964), p. 30.

CHAPTER EIGHT: RIGHTS AND RESISTANCE

1. From the preface to a reprint of Thomas Bradbury, *The Ass: Or, The Serpent* (1712) (Boston, 1768).

2. *See generally* Edward S. Corwin, *The "Higher Law" Background of American Constitutional Law* (Ithaca, N.Y.: Cornell University Press, 1955).
3. James Bryce, *Studies in History and Jurisprudence* (New York: Books for Libraries Press, 1968), p. 599.
4. Carl L. Becker, *The Declaration of Independence: A Study in the History of Political Ideas* (New York: Vintage Books, 1958), p. 51.
5. Corwin, *op. cit.*, p. 59.
6. Becker, *op. cit.*, p. 42.
7. *Ibid.*, pp. 43-44.
8. Clinton Rossiter, *The Seedtime of the Republic: The Origin of the American Tradition of Political Liberty* (New York: Harcourt, Brace, 1953), p. 133.
9. *Ibid.*, p. 134.
10. Corwin, *op. cit.*, pp. 15-16.
11. *Ibid.*, p. 16.
12. As quoted by Rossiter, *op. cit.*, pp. 363-364.
13. *Ibid.*, p. 365.
14. *Ibid.*, p. 366.
15. *Ibid.*
16. *Ibid. See generally* Corwin, *op. cit.*
17. *Ibid.* (emphasis in original).
18. *See, for example,* John W. Whitehead, *The Second American Revolution* (Elgin, Ill.: David C. Cook, 1982), pp. 99-100.
19. Donald S. Lutz, *The Relative Influence of European Writers on Late Eighteenth-Century American Political Thought,* American Political Science Review, Vol. 78 (1982), p. 193.
20. *See* Whitehead, *The Second American Revolution, op. cit.*, pp. 30-32.
21. William Blackstone, *Commentaries on the Laws of England* (1755-1765), Vol. 1 (Philadelphia: J. B. Lippincott, 1898), pp. 39-40 (emphasis in original).
22. Rossiter, *op. cit.*, p. 369.
23. *Ibid.*
24. *Ibid.*, p. 370 (emphasis supplied).
25. *Ibid.*, p. 370.
26. *Ibid.*, p. 371 (emphasis supplied).
27. *Ibid.*, p. 372.
28. *Ibid.*
29. *Regulation of the University of Virginia*, Chap. 2, Section 1 (October 4, 1824).
30. J. O. Wilson, *Public Schools of Washington*, Vol. 1 (Washington, D.C.: Columbia Historical Society, 1897), p. 5.
31. *Ibid.*, p. 9.
32. Rossiter, *op. cit.*, p. 374.
33. Eugen Rosenstock-Huessy, *Out of Revolution* (New York: William Morrow, 1938), p. 648 (emphasis in original).
34. Rossiter, *op. cit.*, p. 375 (emphasis in original).
35. *Ibid.*, pp. 375-376.
36. John Dickinson, *Writings*, Vol. 1 (Philadelphia: The Historical Society of Pennsylvania, 1895), p. 262 (emphasis in original).

37. Alexander Hamilton, *Works,* Vol. II (New York: Charles S. Francis, 1851), p. 80.
38. Rossiter, *op. cit.,* p. 377.
39. Thomas Jefferson, *The Papers of Thomas Jefferson,* Vol. I (Princeton: Princeton University Press, 1950), p. 135.
40. Rossiter, *op. cit.,* p. 379.
41. *Ibid.*
42. *See generally* Howard Mumford Jones, *The Pursuit of Happiness* (Cambridge: Harvard University Press, 1953).
43. Blackstone, *op. cit.,* p. 41.
44. Dickinson, *op. cit.,* p. 262 (emphasis in original).
45. As quoted by Rossiter, *op. cit.,* p. 392.
46. *Ibid.,* p. 394.
47. *Ibid.,* p. 395.
48. *Ibid.* (emphasis in original).
49. *Ibid.*
50. *Ibid.,* p. 397.

CHAPTER NINE: A NEW ORDER FOR THE AGES

1. William Stevens Perry, *The Faith of the Signers of the Declaration of Independence* (Tarrytown, N.Y.: William Abbatt, 1926), p. 223.
2. *Ibid.*
3. *Ibid.,* p. 228.
4. Christopher F. Mooney, *Religion and the American Dream: The Search For Freedom Under God* (Philadelphia: Westminster Press, 1977), p. 18.
5. *Journals of the Continental Congress,* Vol. V (August 17, 1776), pp. 517-518.
6. As quoted by Hannah Arendt, *On Revolution* (New York: Viking Press, 1965), p. 15.
7. Mooney, *op. cit.,* pp. 18-19.
8. As quoted by Ernest Lee Tuveson, *Redeemer Nation: The Idea of America's Millennial Role* (Chicago: University of Chicago Press, 1968), p. vii.
9. *Ibid.*
10. *Ibid.,* pp. vii-viii.
11. *Ibid.,* pp. viii-ix.
12. As quoted by Tuveson, *op. cit.,* p. ix.
13. *Ibid.,* pp. ix, x (emphasis in original).
14. *Ibid.,* p. x.
15. *Ibid.*
16. *Ibid.*
17. Harry S. Stout, *The New England Soul: Preaching and Religious Culture in Colonial New England* (New York: Cambridge University Press, 1986), p. 8.
18. *Ibid.*
19. As quoted by Nathan O. Hatch, *The Sacred Cause of Liberty: Republican Thought and the Millennium in Revolutionary New England* (New Haven: Yale University Press, 1977), p. 21.
20. *Ibid.*

21. *Ibid.*, p. 22.
22. *Ibid.*
23. *Ibid.*
24. *Ibid.*
25. Stout, *op. cit.*, p. 8.
26. Hatch, *op. cit.*, p. 60.
27. *Ibid.*, p. 61.
28. *Ibid.*, p. 88.
29. *Ibid.*
30. *Ibid.*, p. 22.
31. *Ibid.*
32. *Ibid.*, pp. 22-23.

CHAPTER TEN: A CIVIL RELIGION

1. Robert N. Bellah, "Civil Religion in America," *Daedalus*, Vol. 96 (1967), p. 1.
2. Kenneth S. Kantzer, "American Civil Religion," *Christianity Today* (July 13, 1984), pp. 14-15.
3. *Ibid.*, p. 15.
4. Robert N. Bellah, *The Broken Covenant: American Civil Religion in Time of Trial* (New York: Seabury Press, 1975), p. 3.
5. Kantzer, *op. cit.*, p. 14.
6. *Inaugural Addresses of the Presidents of the United States From George Washington (1789) to John F. Kennedy (1961)* (Washington, D.C.: United States Government Printing Office, 1961), p. 267.
7. *Ibid.*, p. 270.
8. Bellah, "Civil Religion in America," *op. cit.*, p. 4.
9. *Ibid.*
10. *Inaugural Addresses of the Presidents, op. cit.*, p. 269.
11. Bellah, *op. cit.*, p. 5.
12. *Inaugural Addresses of the Presidents, op. cit.*, pp. 1-4.
13. Bellah, *op. cit.*, p. 7 (emphasis supplied).
14. *See generally* Harry S. Stout, *The New England Soul: Preaching and Religious Culture in Colonial New England* (New York: Cambridge University Press, 1986).
15. *Inaugural Addresses of the Presidents, op. cit.*, p. 21.
16. Bellah, *op. cit.*, p. 8.
17. *Ibid.*
18. *Ibid.*
19. Benjamin Franklin, *Autobiography* (New York: Putnam, 1942), p. 185.
20. *Ibid.*, p. 223.
21. As quoted by A. James Reichley, *Religion in American Public Life* (Washington, D.C.: Brookings Institution, 1985), p. 101.
22. *Ibid.* (emphasis in original).
23. As quoted by Anson Phelps Stokes, *Church and State in the United States*, Vol. 1 (New York: Harper Brothers, 1950), p. 512.
24. Bellah, *op. cit.*, p. 9. *See also* Sanford Levinson, *"The Constitution" in American Civil Religion*, Supreme Court Review (1979), p. 123.

25. Sidney Mead, *The Lively Experiment* (New York: Harper and Row, 1963), p. 12.
26. As quoted by Arthur Lehman Goodhart in, "Lincoln and the Law," *Lincoln and the Gettysburg Address,* Allen Nevins, ed. (Urbana, Ill.: University of Illinois Press, 1964), p. 39.
27. *Ibid.,* p. 10.
28. *Ibid.,* "On the Gettysburg Address," pp. 88-89.
29. Bellah, *op. cit.,* p. 10.
30. Quoted by George Sherwood Eddy, *The Kingdom of God and the American Dream* (New York: Harper and Row, 1941), p. 162.
31. William Lloyd Warner, *American Life* (Chicago: University of Chicago Press, 1962), pp. 8-9.
32. Bellah, *op. cit.,* p. 11.
33. Alexis de Tocqueville, *Democracy in America,* Vol. I (New York: Vintage Books, 1954), p. 311.
34. *Ibid.,* p. 436.
35. Bellah, *op. cit.,* p. 13.
36. Harold Berman, *The Interaction of Law and Society* (New York: Abingdon Press, 1974), pp. 67-68.
37. *Ibid.,* p. 72.
38. Crane Brinston, John B. Christopher and Rogert Lee Wolff, *A History of Civilization,* Vol. 2, 2nd ed. (Englewood Cliffs, N.J.: Prentice-Hall, 1963), p. 484.
39. Bellah, *The Broken Covenant, op. cit.,* p. ix.
40. *Ibid.,* p. x.
41. *See generally* John W. Whitehead, *The End of Man* (Westchester, Ill.: Crossway Books, 1986).
42. Bellah, *op. cit.,* p. xiv.

CHAPTER ELEVEN: THE SECULAR DREAM

1. *See generally* Frances FitzGerald, *Cities on a Hill: A Journey Through Contemporary American Cultures* (New York: Simon and Schuster, 1986).
2. *See generally* Harvey Cox, *The Secular City* (New York: Macmillan, 1965).
3. Theodore C. Blegen, ed., *Land of Their Choice* (St. Paul: University of Minnesota Press, 1955), p. vi.
4. *Ibid.*
5. Letter from Gjert G. Hovland, at Kendall Settlement, New York, to Torjuls A. Maeland, April 22, 1835, in Blegen, *op. cit.,* pp. 21-22.
6. Robert Benne and Philip Hefner, *Defining America: A Christian Critique of the American Dream* (Philadelphia: Fortress Press, 1974), pp. 21-22.
7. Perry Miller, "Errand into the Wilderness," *Puritanism and the American Experience,* Michael McGiffert, ed. (Reading, Mass.: Addison-Wesley, 1969), p. 101.
8. H. Richard Niebuhr, *The Kingdom of God in America* (New York: Harper Torchbooks, 1957), p. 69.

9. *See generally* John W. Whitehead, *The Second American Revolution* (Elgin, Ill.: David C. Cook, 1982).

10. *See generally* Charles Norman Fay, *Rugged Individualism* (Cambridge, Mass.: Cosmos, 1929). *See also* George B. Cutten, "Rugged Individualism or Rugged Collectivism," convocation address delivered at Colgate University on September 20, 1934, reprinted in *Vital Speeches,* Vol. 1 (New York: The City News Publishing Company, 1934), pp. 70-72; Charles A. Beard, "The Myth of the Rugged Individualism," *Harper's Magazine,* Vol. 164 (December, 1931), pp. 13-22.

11. *See, for example,* Roderick Nash, *Wilderness and the American Mind,* rev. ed. (New Haven: Yale University Press, 1973).

12. Blegen, *op. cit.,* p. 6.

13. *See, for example,* Martin Luther King, "The American Dream," *Negro History Bulletin,* Vol. 31 (May 1968), pp. 10-15.

14. John W. Whitehead, *The Stealing of America* (Westchester, Ill.: Crossway Books, 1983), p. 16.

15. *Ibid.,* p. 14.

16. *The Presidents Speak: Inaugural Addresses of the Presidents* (New York: Holt, Rinehart and Winston, 1969), p. 281.

17. Letter from Gjert G. Hovland, at Kendall Settlement, New York, to Torjuls A. Maeland, April 22, 1835, in Blegen, *op. cit.,* pp. 21-22.

18. *See, for example,* R. H. Tawney, *Religion and the Rise of Capitalism* (New York: Pelican Books, 1938); Kemper Fullerton, *Calvinism and Capitalism,* Harvard Theological Review (July 1928).

19. Blaine Taylor, *The Success Ethic and the Shattered American Dream* (Washington, D.C.: Acropolis Books, 1976), pp. 17-18.

20. *See* John Dunn, *The Political Thought of John Locke: An Historical Account of the Argument of the 'Two Treatises of Government'* (Cambridge: Cambridge University Press, 1969), pp. 245-261.

21. Taylor, *op. cit.,* p. 24.

22. *See generally* Frederick Jackson Turner, *The Significance of the Frontier in American History* (Washington, D.C.: GPO, 1894).

23. Taylor, *op. cit.,* p. 19.

24. For a popular modern expression of this view, *see* Peter Marshall and David Manuel, *The Light and the Glory* (Old Tappan, N.J.: Revell, 1977). *Also, see generally* Conrad Cherry, ed., *God's New Israel: Religious Interpretation of American Destiny* (Englewood Cliffs, N.J.: Prentice-Hall, 1971).

25. Ernest Lee Tuveson, *Redeemer Nation: The Idea of America's Millennial Role* (Chicago: University of Chicago Press, 1968), p. 102.

26. *See generally* Frederick Merk, *Manifest Destiny and Mission in American History* (New York: Knopf, 1963). *Also see* Tuveson, *op. cit.,* pp. 91-136.

CHAPTER TWELVE: ADAM REDUX

1. *See* R. W. B. Lewis, *The American Adam: Innocence, Tragedy and Tradition in the Nineteenth Century* (Chicago: University of Chicago Press, 1955).

2. *See generally* Christopher Lasch, *The Culture of Narcissism: American Life in an Age of Diminishing Expectations* (New York: Warner Books, 1979).

3. *See generally* John W. Whitehead, *The End of Man* (Westchester, Ill.: Crossway Books, 1986) and John W. Whitehead, *The Stealing of America* (Westchester, Ill.: Crossway Books, 1983).

4. Whitehead, *The End of Man, op. cit.*, p. 17.

5. Michael Harrington, *The Politics at God's Funeral: The Spiritual Crisis of Western Civilization* (New York: Holt, Rinehart and Winston, 1983), p. 1.

6. George Gallup, Jr., *Forecast 2000: George Gallup, Jr., Predicts the Future of America* (New York: William Morrow, 1984), p. 152.

7. *Ibid.*, p. 153.

8. Harrington, *op. cit.*, pp. 10-11.

9. Neil Postman, *Amusing Ourselves to Death: Public Discourse in the Age of Show Business* (New York: Viking Press, 1985), p. 117.

10. Jacques Ellul, *The Political Illusion* (New York: Vintage Press, 1972), p. 9.

11. Bertram Gross, *Friendly Fascism: The New Face of Power in America* (New York: M. Evans, 1980), p. 124.

12. *See, for example,* Mark A. Noll, Nathan O. Hatch, and George M. Marsden, *The Search for Christian America* (Westchester, Ill.: Crossway Books, 1983), pp. 70-106.

13. *See* John W. Whitehead, *The Second American Revolution* (Elgin, Ill.: David C. Cook, 1982), pp. 145-160. *Also see* John W. Whitehead, *The Right to Picket and the Freedom of Public Discourse* (Westchester, Ill.: Crossway Books, 1984).

14. Quentin Skinner, *The Foundations of Modern Political Thought: The Age of Reformation,* Vol. II (Cambridge: Cambridge University Press, 1978), p. 207.

15. Junius Brutus, *A Defence of Liberty Against Tyrants: A Translation of the Vindiciae contra Tyrannos* (1579) (London: G. Bell and Sons, 1924).

16. Skinner, *op. cit.*, p. 230.

17. Michael Walzer, *Exodus and Revolution* (New York: Basic Books, 1985), p. 12 (emphasis in original).

18. Lasch, *op. cit.*, p. 28.

19. *Ibid.*

20. "Birthrate in U.S. Remains Below Replacement Level," *Washington Post* (October 27, 1986), p. A6.

21. *Ibid.*

22. *Ibid.*

23. Germaine Greer, *Sex and Destiny* (New York: Harper and Row, 1984), p. 444.

24. As quoted by Catherine O'Neill, "No Tomorrow: Teen Suicide in America," *Washington Post Health Magazine* (April 23, 1986), p. 12.

SELECT BIBLIOGRAPHY

As the heading suggests, this bibliography makes no pretense to be exhaustive. I have listed only the works I have actually used and cited in the text and/or referred to in the process of writing this book. Even so, for a subject as complex and multidimensional as set forth in the text, it is impossible to remember, let alone do full justice to, all the writings which have helped to form my opinions.

Aaron, Richard I. *John Locke* [1937]. Oxford: Clarendon Press, 1955.

Adams, James T. "Our American Dream." *Catholic World*. November 1931.

Adams, John. *Works*. Vol. I. Boston: Little, Brown, 1856.

_____. *Works*. Vol. X. New York: AMS Press, 1971.

_____. *Papers of John Adams*. Robert J. Taylor, ed. Vol. IV. Cambridge: Belknap Press, 1979.

Agar, Herbert. *The Price of Union*. Boston: Houghton Mifflin, 1950.

Ahlstrom, Sydney. *A Religious History of the American People*. New Haven: Yale University Press, 1972.

Allen, Walter. *The Urgent West: The American Dream and Modern Man*. New York: E. P. Dutton & Co., 1969.

Andrew, Brother. *The Ethics of Smuggling*. Wheaton, Ill.: Tyndale House, 1979.

Andrist, Ralph K., ed. *George Washington: A Biography in His Own Words*. 2 vols. New York: Newsweek, 1972.

Angle, Paul M. *By These Words*. New York: Rand McNally, 1954.

_____, ed. *Abraham Lincoln's Speeches and Letters, 1832-1865*. 1907. Reprint. London: J. M. Dent & Sons, 1957.

Arendt, Hannah. *On Revolution*. New York: Viking Press, 1965.

Aristotle. *Politics*. Cambridge: Harvard University Press, 1932.

Ascherson, Neal, ed. *The French Revolution: Extracts from the Times, 1789-1794*. London: Times Books, 1975.

Bailyn, Bernard. *The Ideological Origins of the American Revolution*. Cambridge: Belknap Press, 1967.

Bailyn, Bernard, David Brian Davis, David Herbert Donald, John L. Thomas, Robert H. Wiebe, and Gordon S. Wood. *The Great Republic: A History of the American People*. Boston: Little, Brown, 1977.

Bainton, Roland. *The Travail of Religious Liberty*. Hamden, Conn.: Shoe String Press, 1971.

Baldwin, Alice M. *The New England Clergy and the American Revolution*. New York: Frederick Ungar, 1928.

Bartlett, Irving H. *Daniel Webster*. New York: W. W. Norton, 1978.

Bass, Archer B. *Protestantism in the United States*. New York: Thomas Y. Crowell, 1929.

Bates, M. Searle. *Religious Liberty: An Inquiry*. New York: Harper and Brothers, 1945.

Bauer, P. T. *Equality, the Third World and Economic Delusion*. Cambridge: Harvard University Press, 1981.

Baumer, Franklin L. *Modern European Thought*. New York: Macmillan, 1977.

Beard, Charles A. "The Myth of the Rugged Individualism." *Harper's Magazine*. Vol. 164. December 1931.

Becker, Carl. *The Eve of the Revolution*. New Haven: Yale University Press, 1918.

_____. *The Declaration of Independence: A Study in the History of Political Ideas* [1922]. New York: Vintage Books, 1958.

———. *Beginnings of the American People* [1915]. Ithaca, N.Y.: Cornell University Press, 1966.

Bellah, Robert. "Civil Religion in America." *Daedalus.* Winter 1967.

———. *The Broken Covenant: American Civil Religion in Time of Trial.* New York: Seabury Press, 1975.

———. "Civil Religion: The Sacred and the Political in American Life." *Psychology Today.* January 1976.

Bellamy, Francis Rufus. *The Private Life of George Washington.* New York: Thomas Y. Crowell, 1951.

Benne, Robert and Philip Hefner. *Defining America: A Christian Critique of the American Dream.* Philadelphia: Fortress Press, 1974.

Berman, Harold. *The Interaction of Law and Society.* New York: Abindgon Press, 1974.

Bigelow, William Frederick. "The American Dream." *Good Housekeeping.* February 1941.

"Birthrate in U.S. Remains Below Replacement Level." *Washington Post.* October 27, 1986.

Blackstone, William. *Commentaries on the Laws of England* [1755-1765]. 2 vols. Philadelphia: J. B. Lippincott, 1866.

———. *Commentaries on the Laws of England* [1755-1765]. Vol. I. Philadelphia: J. B. Lippincott, 1898.

Blamires, Harry. *The Christian Mind.* Ann Arbor: Servant Books, 1963.

Blegin, Theodore C., ed. *Land of Their Choice.* St. Paul: University of Minnesota Press, 1955.

Boorstin, Daniel J. *The Genius of American Politics.* Chicago: University of Chicago Press, 1955.

———. *The Americans: The Colonial Experience.* New York: Vintage Books, 1958.

———. *Image; or, What Happened to the American Dream.* New York: Atheneum, 1962.

———. *The Americans: The Democratic Experience.* New York: Random House, 1973.

———. *The Image: A Guide to Pseudo-Events in America.* New York: Atheneum, 1980.

Borisov, Vadim. "Personality and National Awareness." *From Under the Rubble.* Boston: Little, Brown, 1975.

Bosworth, Allan R. *America's Concentration Camps.* New York: Bantam Books, 1968.

Bourdeaux, Michael and Michael Rowe. *May One Believe—in Russia?* London: Darton, Longman & Todd, 1980.

Bowen, Catherine Drinker. *John Adams and the American Revolution.* Boston: Little, Brown, 1950.

_____. *Miracle at Philadelphia.* Boston: Little, Brown, 1966.

_____. *Yankee from Olympus.* Boston: Little, Brown, 1944.

Bowers, Claude G. *Jefferson in Power.* Boston: Houghton Mifflin, 1936.

Bradbury, Ray. *Fahrenheit 451.* New York: Ballantine Books, 1979.

Bradley, Harold Whitman. *The United States, 1492-1877.* New York: Charles Scribner's Sons, 1972.

Bradley, Thomas. *The Ass: Or, The Serpent* [1712]. Boston, 1768.

Brant, Irving. *James Madison: The Father of the Constitution, 1787-1800.* Indianapolis: Bobbs-Merrill, 1950.

Bridenbaugh, Carl. *Mitre and Sceptre: Transatlantic Faiths, Ideas, Personalities, and Politics, 1689-1775.* New York: Oxford University Press, 1962.

Brinston, Crane, John Christopher and Robert Lee Wolff. *A History of Civilization.* Englewood Cliffs, N.J.: Prentice-Hall, 1960.

Brodie, Fawn M. *Thomas Jefferson: An Intimate History.* New York: W. W. Norton, 1974.

Brogan, Hugh. *The American Civil War: Extracts from the Times, 1860-1865.* London: Times Books, 1975.

Broom, Leonard and Philip Selznick. *Sociology: A Text with Adapted Readings.* 4th ed. New York: Harper and Row, 1968.

Brown, Harold O. J. *The Reconstruction of the Republic.* New Rochelle, N.Y.: Arlington House, 1977.

_____. *Heresies.* Garden City, N.Y.: Doubleday, 1984.

Brown, Robert E. *Middle-Class Democracy and the Revolution in Massachusetts, 1691-1780.* Ithaca: Cornell University Press, 1955.

Brown, William R. *Imagemaker: Will Rogers and the American Dream.* Columbia, Mo.: University of Missouri Press, 1970.

Bryce, James. *Studies in History and Jurisprudence.* New York: Books for Libraries Press, 1968.

Bullock, Alan. *Hitler: A Study in Tyranny.* Rev. ed. New York: Harper and Row, 1962.

Burgess, Anthony. *A Clockwork Orange.* New York: W. W. Norton, 1963.

Burke, Edmund and Thomas Paine. *Reflections on the Revolution and the Rights of Man.* Garden City, N.Y.: Dolphin Books, 1961.

Burnham, David. *The Rise of the Computer State.* New York: Random House, 1983.

Burnham, James. *Congress and the American Tradition.* Chicago: Regnery, 1959.

Calvin, John. *Institutes of the Christian Religion* [1536-1559]. Grand Rapids, Mich.: Eerdmans, 1953.

_____. *The Institutes of the Christian Religion* [1536-1559]. 2 vols. Reprint. Philadelphia: Westminster Press, 1960.

Campbell, Norine Dickson. *Patrick Henry: Patriot and Statesman.* Old Greenwich, Conn.: Devin-Adair, 1969.

Camus, Albert. *The Rebel.* Anthony Bower, trans. New York: Knopf, 1969.

Carroll, Peter N. *Puritanism and the Wilderness.* New York: Columbia University Press, 1969.

Chabannes, Jacques. *Saint Augustine.* Garden City, N.Y.: Doubleday, 1962.

Cherry, Conrad, ed. *God's New Israel: Religious Interpretation of American Destiny.* Englewood Cliffs, N.J.: Prentice-Hall, 1971.

Chesterton, Gilbert K. *What I Saw in America.* New York: Dodd, Mead, 1922.

Clark, Kenneth. *Civilisation: A Personal View.* New York: Harper and Row, 1969.

Cohn, Norman. *The Pursuit of the Millennium.* New York: Oxford University Press, 1970.

Coke, Edward. *Institutes of the Laws of England* [1628-1644]. 4 vols. 11th ed. London: Eliz. Nutt and R. Goslang (assigns of E. Sayer), 1719.

Cole, Arthur C. *The Irrepressible Conflict, 1850-1865.* Chicago: Quadrangle Books, 1971.

Collingwood, R. G. *The Idea of Nature.* Oxford: Clarendon Press, 1945.

Commager, Henry Steele. *Jefferson, Nationalism, and the Enlightenment.* New York: George Braziller, 1975.

_____. *The Empire of Reason.* Garden City, N.Y.: Anchor Press-Doubleday, 1977.

Corwin, Edward S. *The "Higher Law" Background of American Constitutional Law*. Ithaca, N.Y.: Cornell University Press, 1955.

Cotham, Perry C. *Politics, Americanism, and Christianity*. Grand Rapids, Mich.: Baker Book House, 1976.

Cousins, Norman. *In God We Trust*. New York: Harper and Brothers, 1958.

Cox, Harvey. *The Secular City: Secularization and Urbanization in Theological Perspective*. New York: Macmillan, 1965.

_____. *The Seduction of the Spirit*. New York: Simon and Schuster, 1973.

_____. *Religion in the Secular City: Toward a Postmodern Theology*. New York: Simon and Schuster, 1984.

Crick, Francis. *Of Molecules and Men*. Seattle: University of Washington Press, 1967.

Cunliffe, Marcus. *George Washington: Man and Monument*. New York: Mentor Books, 1958.

Cushing, Harry Alonzo, ed. *The Writings of Samuel Adams*. 4 vols. New York: Octagon Books, 1968.

Cutten, George B. "Rugged Individualism or Rugged Collectivism." Convocation address delivered at Colgate University on September 20, 1934. Reprinted in *Vital Speeches*. Vol. I. New York: The City News Publishing Company, 1934.

Darwin, Charles. *Autobiography*. New York: Dover Publications, 1958.

_____. *The Descent of Man*. London: John Murray, 1871.

_____. *The Illustrated Origin of Species*. New York: Hill & Wang, 1979.

_____. *The Origin of Species by Means of Natural Selection or the Preservation of Favoured Races in the Struggle for Life* [1859]. New York: D. Appleton, 1872.

_____. *The Origin of Species by Means of Natural Selection or the Preservation of Favoured Races in the Struggle for Life* [1859]. L. Valorium, ed. Philadelphia: University of Pennsylvania Press, 1959.

Davis, Burke. *George Washington and the American Revolution*. New York: Random House, 1975.

Dewar, Douglas and H. S. Shelton. *Is Evolution Proved?* London: Hollis & Carter, 1947.

Dewey, John. *A Common Faith*. New Haven: Yale University Press, 1934.

Dickinson, John. *Writings*. Vol. I. Philadelphia: The Historical Society of Pennsylvania, 1895.

Donahue, Phil. *The Human Animal*. New York: Simon and Schuster, 1985.

Donovan, Frank. *Mr. Madison's Constitution*. New York: Dodd, Mead, 1965.

Dostoyevski, Fyodor. *The Brothers Karamazov*. New York: Bantam Books, 1970.

Dotson, Bob. *". . . In Pursuit of The American Dream."* New York: Atheneum, 1985.

Dreisbach, Daniel L. *Late Reformation Resistance Theology and Its Revival in Current American Politics*. A paper presented to the Symposium on American Politics, Social Studies Centre, Oxford University. February 23, 1983.

Drucker, Peter F. *The Future of Industrial Man*. New York: John Day, 1942.

———. *The Unseen Revolution*. New York: Harper and Row, 1976.

Drummond, Henry. *Natural Law in the Spiritual World*. New York: James Pott, 1887.

Dumbauld, Edward. *The Declaration of Independence and What It Means Today*. Norman, Okla.: University of Oklahoma Press, 1950.

Dunn, John. *The Political Thought of John Locke: An Historical Account of the Argument of the 'Two Treatises of Government.'* Cambridge: Cambridge University Press, 1969.

———. *"The Politics of Locke in England and America in the Eighteenth Century." John Locke: Problems and Perspectives*. John W. Yolton, ed. Cambridge: Cambridge University Press, 1969.

Dunning, William Archibald. *A History of Political Theories: From Luther to Montesquieu*. New York: Macmillan, 1920.

Durant, Will. *The Story of Philosophy*. New York: Simon and Schuster, 1961.

Durant, Will and Ariel. *The Life of Greece*. New York: Simon and Schuster, 1939.

———. *The Age of Faith*. New York: Simon and Schuster, 1950.

———. *The Story of Civilization*. 11 vols. New York: Simon and Schuster, 1954-1975.

———. *The Age of Reason Begins*. New York: Simon and Schuster, 1961.

_____. *The Lessons of History.* New York: Simon and Schuster, 1968.

_____. *The Age of Napoleon: A History of European Civilization from 1789 to 1815.* New York: Simon and Schuster, 1975.

Eddy, George Sherwood. *The Kingdom of God and the American Dream.* New York: Harper and Row, 1941.

Einstein, Albert. *Out of My Later Years.* London: Thames and Hudson, 1950.

_____. *Ideas and Opinions.* New York: Bonanza Books, 1954.

Ellul, Jacques. *The Technological Society.* New York: Vintage Books, 1964.

_____. *The Theological Foundation of Law.* New York: Seabury Press, 1969.

_____. *The Meaning of the City.* Grand Rapids, Mich.: Eerdmans, 1970.

_____. *The Political Illusion.* New York: Vintage Press, 1972.

Emery, Noemie. *Washington: A Biography.* New York: G. P. Putnam's Sons, 1976.

Erlich, Paul. *The Population Bomb.* New York: Ballantine Books, 1968.

Esses, Rev. Michael. *The Next Visitor to Planet Earth.* Plainfield, N.J.: Logos International, 1975.

Evans, Christopher. *The Micro Millennium.* New York: Washington Square Press, 1979.

Fantel, Hans. *William Penn: Apostle of Dissent.* New York: William Morrow, 1974.

Fay, Charles Norman. *Rugged Individualism.* Cambridge, Mass.: Cosmos, 1929.

Ferrero, Guglielmo and Corrado Barbagallo. *A Short History of Rome.* 2 vols. New York: Knickerbocker Press, 1919.

Figgis, Rev. J. Neville. "Political Thought in the Sixteenth Century." *The Cambridge Modern History: The Wars of Religion.* Vol. III. Chap. XII. New York: Macmillan, 1934.

Fisher, Gene and Glen Chambers. *The Revolution Myth.* Greenville, S.C.: Bob Jones University Press, 1981.

Fitzgerald, Frances. *Cities on a Hill: A Journey Through Contemporary American Cultures.* New York: Simon and Schuster, 1986.

Fitzpatrick, James K. *Builders of the American Dream.* New Rochelle, N.Y.: Arlington House, 1977.

Flake, Carol. *Redemptorama: Culture, Politics, and the New*

Evangelicalism. New York: Anchor Press, 1984.

Flexner, James Thomas. *George Washington.* 4 vols. Boston: Little, Brown, 1965-1972.

_____. *Washington: The Indispensable Man.* Boston: Little, Brown, 1974.

_____. *The Young Hamilton.* Boston: Little, Brown, 1978.

Foner, Eric. *Tom Paine and Revolutionary America.* New York: Oxford University Press, 1976.

Foner, Phillip S., ed. *Basic Writings of Thomas Jefferson.* Garden City, N.Y.: Halcyon House, 1950.

_____. *The Life and Major Writings of Thomas Paine.* Secaucus, N.J.: Citadel Press, 1974.

Ford, Paul Leicester, ed. *The Writings of Thomas Jefferson.* 10 vols. New York: G. P. Putnam's Sons, 1892-1899.

Ford, Thomas R. *The Revolutionary Theme in Contemporary America.* Lexington, Ky.: University of Kentucky Press, 1965.

Forester, Norman. *Image in America.* Notre Dame, Ind.: University of Notre Dame Press, 1962.

Foster, Herbert D. *International Calvinism Through Locke and the Revolution of 1688.* American Historical Review. Vol. 32, 1927.

Franklin, Benjamin. *Autobiography.* New York: Putnam, 1942.

_____. *The Papers of Benjamin Franklin.* Vol. I. New Haven: Yale University Press, 1959.

Freeman, David Hugh. *A Philosophical Study of Religion.* Nutley, N.J.: Craig Press, 1964.

Freud, Sigmund. *Moses and Monotheism.* New York: Knopf, 1949.

_____. *Civilization and Its Discontents.* New York: Doubleday, 1958.

_____. *The Future of an Illusion.* Garden City, N.Y.: Anchor Books, 1964.

Fullerton, Kemper. *Calvinism and Capitalism.* Harvard Theological Review. July 1928.

Gabriel, Ralph Henry. *The Course of American Democratic Thought.* 2d ed. New York: John Wiley and Sons, 1956.

Galbraith, John Kenneth. *The Affluent Society.* Boston: Houghton Mifflin, 1958.

_____. *The Age of Uncertainty.* Boston: Houghton Mifflin, 1977.

Galbraith, John Kenneth and M. S. Randhawa. *The New Indus-*

trial State. Boston: Houghton Mifflin, 1967.

Gallup, George, Jr. *Forecast 2000: George Gallup, Jr., Predicts the Future of America.* New York: William Morrow, 1984.

Gaucher, Roland. *Opposition in the U.S.S.R., 1917-1967.* New York: Funk and Wagnalls, 1969.

Gay, Peter. *The Enlightenment: An Interpretation—The Rise of Modern Paganism.* New York: Knopf, 1967.

———. *The Enlightenment: An Interpretation—The Science of Freedom.* New York: Knopf, 1969.

Gentz, Friedrich. "The French and American Revolutions Compared." *Three Revolutions.* S. T. Possony, ed. John Quincy Adams, trans. Chicago: Regnery, 1959.

Gibbon, Edward. *The Decline and Fall of the Roman Empire* [1776-1788]. 6 vols. Reprint. New York: Dutton, 1910.

Gilder, George. *Sexual Suicide.* New York: Quadrangle-New York Times, 1973.

———. *Naked Nomads.* New York: Quadrangle-New York Times, 1974.

———. *Wealth and Poverty.* New York: Basic Books, 1981.

Goebel, Julius, Jr., ed. *The Law Practice of Alexander Hamilton.* New York: Columbia University Press, 1964.

Goodhart, Arthur Lehman. "Lincoln and the Law." *Lincoln and the Gettysburg Address.* Allen Nevins, ed. Urbana, Ill.: University of Illinois Press, 1964.

Gorman, Michael J. *Abortion and the Early Church.* Downers Grove, Ill.: InterVarsity Press, 1982.

Grant, Michael. *History of Rome.* New York: Charles Scribner's Sons, 1978.

Greene, Jack P. and William G. McLaughlin. *Preachers and Politicians: Two Essays on the Origins of the American Revolution.* Worchester: American Antiquarian Society, 1977.

Greer, Germaine. *Sex and Destiny.* New York: Harper and Row, 1984.

Grimal, Pierre. *The Civilization of Rome.* New York: Simon and Schuster, 1963.

Gross, Bertram. *Friendly Fascism: The New Face of Power in America.* New York: M. Evans, 1980.

Grunwald, Henry. "The Morning After the Fourth: Have We Kept Our Promise?" *Time.* July 14, 1975.

Guinness, Os. *The Dust of Death.* Downers Grove, Ill.: InterVarsity Press, 1973.

Haile, H. G. *Luther: An Experiment in Biography.* New York: Doubleday, 1980.

Hall, Thomas Cuming. *The Religious Background of American Culture.* Boston: Little, Brown, 1930.

Hamilton, Alexander. *Works.* Vol. II. New York: Charles S. Francis, 1851.

Handy, Robert T. *A Christian America: Protestant Hopes and Historical Realities.* London: Oxford University Press, 1971.

Harrington, Michael. *The Politics at God's Funeral: The Spiritual Crisis of Western Civilization.* New York: Holt, Rinehart and Winston, 1983.

Harrison, Frank Mott. *John Bunyan.* 1928. Reprint. London: Banner of Truth Trust, 1964.

Hatch, Nathan O. *The Sacred Cause of Liberty: Republican Thought and the Millennium in Revolutionary New England.* New Haven: Yale University Press, 1977.

Hatch, Nathan O. and Mark A. Noll. *The Bible in America: Essays in Cultural History.* New York: Oxford University Press, 1982.

Heidegger, Martin. *Being and Time.* New York: Harper and Row, 1962.

Heilbroner, Robert L. *The Worldly Philosophers.* New York: Simon and Schuster, 1953.

Heimert, Alan and Perry Miller, eds. *The Great Awakening.* Indianapolis: Bobbs-Merrill, 1967.

Herdman, Marie L. *The Story of the United States.* New York: Grossett & Dunlap, 1916.

Hill, Christopher. *The Century of Revolution, 1703-1714.* New York: Nelson, 1961.

Hillel, Marc and Clarissa Henry. *Of Pure Blood.* New York: McGraw-Hill, 1976.

Hillerbrand, Hans J. *The Protestant Reformation.* New York: Walker, 1968.

Howell, Daniel Walker, ed. *The American Whigs.* New York: John Wiley & Sons, 1973.

Howgate, George W. *George Santayana.* New York: A. S. Barnes, 1938.

Hudson, Winthrop S. *Religion in America.* New York: Charles Scribner's Sons, 1973.

Hunt, Frazier. "America Must Dream Again." *Good Housekeeping.* February 1933.

Hunt, Gaillard, ed. *Writings of James Madison.* 9 vols. New York: G. P. Putnam's Sons, 1900-1910.

Huntford, Roland. *The New Totalitarians.* New York: Stein & Day, 1972.

Huxley, Aldous. *Science, Liberty, and Peace.* New York: Harper and Row, 1946.

_____. *The Doors of Perception.* New York: Harper and Row, 1954.

_____. *Heaven and Hell.* New York: Harper and Row, 1956.

_____. *Brave New World* [1932]. New York: Bantam Books, 1968.

Huxley, Julian. "At Random—A Television Preview." *Evolution After Darwin.* Vol. I. Chicago: University of Chicago Press, 1960.

_____, ed. *The Humanist Frame.* New York: Harper and Row, 1962.

Hyams, Edward. *The Millennium Postponed: Socialism from Sir Thomas Moore to Mao Tse-tung.* New York: Taplinger, 1974.

Hyde, Douglas. *Dedication and Leadership.* Notre Dame, Ind.: University of Notre Dame Press, 1966.

Hyman, Harold, M. *A More Perfect Union.* Boston: Houghton Mifflin, 1975.

Inaugural Addresses of the Presidents of the United States from George Washington (1789) to John F. Kennedy (1961). Washington, D.C.: United States Government Printing Office, 1961.

Irving, Washington. *George Washington: A Biography.* 5 vols. Garden City, N.Y.: Doubleday, 1976.

Jaspers, Karl. *Man in the Modern Age.* New York: Doubleday, 1957.

Jefferson, Thomas. *Jefferson Himself.* Bernard Mayo. ed. Boston: Houghton Mifflin, 1942.

_____. *The Papers of Thomas Jefferson.* Vol. I. Princeton: Princeton University Press, 1950.

Jones, Howard Mumford. *The Pursuit of Happiness.* Cambridge: Harvard University Press, 1953.

Jones, R. Ben. *The French Revolution.* London: Minerva Press, 1967.

Journals of the Continental Congress. Vol. V. August 17, 1776.

Jung, C. G. *Collected Works*. Vol. II. Princeton, N.J.: Princeton University Press, 1969.

Kammen, Michael. *A Machine That Would Go of Itself: The Constitution in American Culture*. New York: Knopf, 1986.

Kant, Immanuel. *Critique of Pure Reason* [1781]. Reprint. New York: Wiley, 1943.

Kantzer, Kenneth S. "American Civil Religion." *Christianity Today.* July 13, 1984.

Kauffmann, Walter, trans. *The Portable Nietzsche*. New York: Viking Press, 1968.

Kerkut, G. A. *Implications of Evolution*. New York: Pergamon Press, 1960.

King, Martin Luther. "The American Dream." *Negro History Bulletin*. Vol. 31. May 1968.

Kinnaird, Clark. *George Washington: The Pictorial Biography.* New York: Bonanza Books, 1967.

Kirk, Russel. *The Roots of American Order.* LaSalle, Ill.: Open Court, 1974.

Kline, Mary-Jo, ed. *Alexander Hamilton: A Biography in His Own Words*. New York: Newsweek, 1973.

Koch, G. Adolf. *Religion of the American Enlightenment*. New York: Thomas Y. Crowell, 1968.

Koch, H. W. *Hitler Youth: The Duped Generation*. New York: Ballantine Books, 1972.

Konefsky, Samuel J. *John Marshall and Alexander Hamilton: Architects of the American Constitution*. New York: Macmillan, 1964.

Krajenke, Robert William. *The Psychic Side of the American Dream: Revitalizing the American Spirit*. Virginia Beach, Va.: Christian Science Publishing Company, 1976.

Kramnick, Isaac, ed. *Thomas Paine: Common Sense*. New York: Penguin Books, 1976.

Kuehnelt-Leddihn, Erik von. *Leftism: From de Sade and Marx to Hitler and Marcuse*. New Rochelle, N.Y.: Arlington House, 1974.

Kyemba, Henry. *A State of Blood: The Inside Story of Idi Amin*. New York: Grossett and Dunlap, 1977.

Lamont, Robert J. "Another Look at the American Dream." *Christianity Today.* April 1970.

Lamprecht, Sterling Power. *The Moral and Political Philosophy of John Locke* [1918]. New York: Russell and Russell, 1962.

Laqueur, Walter, ed. *Fascism—A Reader's Guide: Analyses, Interpretations, Bibliography.* Berkeley: University of California Press, 1976.

———. *Terrorism.* Boston: Little, Brown, 1977.

Lasch, Christopher. *The Culture of Narcissism: American Life in an Age of Diminishing Expectations.* New York: Warner Books, 1979.

Laski, Harold J. "Historical Introduction." *Junius Brutus, A Defense of Liberty Against Tyrants: A Translation of the Vindiciae contra Tyrannos.* London: G. Bell and Sons, 1924.

Laslett, Peter. "Introduction." John Locke. *Two Treatises of Civil Government.* Cambridge: Cambridge University Press, 1960.

Leder, Lawrence H., ed. *The Meaning of the American Revolution.* Chicago: Quadrangle Books, 1969.

Lenski, Gerhard. *The Religious Factor: A Sociological Study of Religion's Impact on Politics, Economics and Family Life.* Garden City, N.Y.: Doubleday, 1961.

Lerner, Max. *America as a Civilization.* New York: Simon and Schuster, 1957.

Levinson, Sanford. *"The Constitution" in American Civil Religion.* The Supreme Court Review, 1979.

Lewis, C. S. *The Discarded Image.* New York: Cambridge University Press, 1964.

———. *The Abolition of Man.* New York: Macmillan, 1965.

Lewis, R. W. B. *The American Adam: Innocence, Tragedy, and Tradition in the Nineteenth Century.* Chicago: University of Chicago Press, 1955.

Lewis, Theresa and Luther Luedtke. "The American Dream: A Comprehensive Bibliography." University of Southern California: unpublished, 1975.

Linder, Robert D. and Richard V. Pierard. *Twilight of the Saints: Biblical Christianity in America.* Downers Grove, Ill.: Inter-Varsity Press, 1978.

Locke, John. *An Essay Concerning Human Understanding* [1690]. Alexander Campbell Fraser, ed. 2 vols. New York: Dover, 1959.

———. *On the Reasonableness of Christianity* [1695]. Reprint. Chicago: Henry Regnery, 1965.

———. *Two Treatises of Civil Government* [1690]. Cambridge:

Cambridge University Press, 1970.

Lodge, Henry Cabot. *The Works of Alexander Hamilton.* 12 vols. New York: G. P. Putnam's Sons, 1904.

Lough, John, ed. *Locke's Travels in France, 1675-1679: As Related in His Journals, Correspondence and Other Papers.* Cambridge: Cambridge University Press, 1953.

Lutz, Donald S. *The Relative Influence of European Writers on Late Eighteenth Century American Political Thought.* American Historical Review. Vol. 78, 1984.

MacDonald, Alan. "Death of a Phrase." *Commonweal* 19, April 1934.

Machen, J. Gresham. *The Christian Faith in the Modern World.* Grand Rapids, Mich.: Eerdmans, 1965.

Machiavelli, Niccolo. *The Prince* [1513]. Reprint. New York: Penguin Books, 1961.

Madden, David, ed. *American Dreams, American Nightmares.* Carbondale: Southern Illinois U. Press, 1970.

Malbin, Michael J. *Religion and Politics: The Intentions of the Authors of the First Amendment.* Washington, D.C.: American Enterprise Institute for Public Policy Research, 1978.

Malone, Dumas. *Jefferson and His Time.* 6 vols. Boston: Little, Brown, 1948-1981.

Mannix, Daniel P. *Those About to Die.* New York: Ballantine Books, 1958.

Marcuse, Herbert. *One Dimensional Man.* Boston: Beacon Press, 1964.

Marius, Richard. *Luther: A Biography.* Philadelphia: J. B. Lippincott, 1974.

Marshall, John. *The Life of George Washington.* 2 vols. 2nd ed. Philadelphia: James Crissy, 1835.

Marshall, Peter and David Manuel. *The Light and the Glory.* Old Tappan, N.J.: Revell, 1977.

Marx, Karl, and Friedrich Engels. *The Manifesto of the Communist Party* [1848]. Reprint. San Francisco: China Books, 1965.

May, Henry F. *The Enlightenment in America.* New York: Oxford University Press, 1976.

Mayhew, Jonathan. *A Defense of the Observation on the Charter and Conduct of the Society for the Propagation of the Gospel in Foreign Parts.* Boston, 1763.

McDonald, Forrest. *E Pluribus Unum: The Formation of the*

American Republic, 1776-1790. Boston: Houghton Mifflin, 1965.

―――. *Novus Ordo Seclorum: The Intellectual Origins of the Constitution.* Lawrence, Kan.: University Press of Kansas, 1985.

McLuhan, Marshall. *The Gutenberg Galaxy.* Toronto: University of Toronto Press, 1962.

―――. *Understanding Media: The Extension of Man.* New York: McGraw-Hill, 1964.

―――. "Cybernation and Culture." *The Social Impact of Cybernetics.* New York: Simon and Schuster, 1966.

McManners, John. *The French Revolution and the Church.* New York: Harper and Row, 1969.

Mead, Sidney. *The Lively Experiment.* New York: Harper and Row, 1963.

Merk, Frederick. *Manifest Destiny and Mission in American History.* New York: Knopf, 1963.

Methvin, Eugene H. *The Rise of Radicalism.* New Rochelle, N.Y.: Arlington House, 1973.

Mickleson, Sig. *The Electric Mirror: Politics in an Age of Television.* New York: Dodd, Mead, 1972.

Middelmann, Udo. *Pro-Existence.* Downers Grove, Ill.: InterVarsity Press, 1974.

Miller, John C. *Origins of the American Revolution.* Boston: Little, Brown, 1943.

―――. *The Wolf by the Ears: Thomas Jefferson and Slavery.* New York: Free Press, 1977.

Miller, Perry. *The New England Mind.* New York: Macmillan, 1939.

―――. *The Life of the Mind in America.* London: Victor Gallancz, 1966.

―――. "Errand Into the Wilderness." *Puritanism and the American Experience.* Michael McGiffert, ed. Reading, Mass.: Addison-Wesley, 1969.

Miller, Perry and T. H. Johnson. *The Puritans.* New York: American Book Company, 1938.

Miller, Raymond C., ed. *Twentieth-Century Pessimism and the American Dream.* Westport, Conn.: Greenwood Press, 1961.

Mises, Ludwig von. *Omnipotent Government: The Rise of the State and Total State.* New Rochelle, N.Y.: Arlington House, 1969.

Mitchell, Broadus. *Alexander Hamilton: The Revolutionary Years.* New York: Thomas Y. Crowell, 1970.

Moberly, Sir Walter. *The Crisis in the University.* New York: Macmillan, 1949.

Moellering, Ralph L. "Civil Religion, the Nixon Theology and the Watergate Scandal." *Christian Century.* September 26, 1973.

Monaghan, Patrick. " 'Substantively Due Processing' the Black Population." *Lincoln Review.* Vol. 4 (1983).

Montesquieu, Baron de (Charles de Secondat). *The Spirit of Laws.* 2 vols. Rev. ed. Thomas Nugent, trans. London: George Bell and Sons, 1897.

_____. *The Spirit of Laws.* 2 vols. Rev. ed. Thomas Nugent, trans. New York: Colonial Press, 1899.

Mooney, Christopher F. *Religion and the American Dream: The Search for Freedom Under God.* Philadelphia: Westminster Press, 1977.

Moore, Barrington, Jr. *Social Origins of Dictatorship and Democracy.* Boston: Beacon Press, 1966.

Moorhead, James H. *American Apocalypse: Yankees and Protestants and the Civil War, 1860-1869.* New Haven: Yale University Press, 1978.

Morgan, Edmund, ed. *Puritan Political Ideas, 1558-1794.* Indianapolis: Bobbs-Merrill, 1965.

Morison, Samuel, Henry Commager and William Lauchtenburg. *The Growth of the American Republic.* 2 vols. New York: Oxford University Press, 1980.

Morris, Richard B. *Seven Who Shaped Our Destiny.* New York: Harper and Row, 1973.

_____. *John Jay: The Making of a Revolutionary.* New York: Harper and Row, 1975.

_____, ed. *Encyclopedia of American History* [1953.] New York: Harper and Row, 1976.

Moyers, Bill. "Prudence Reigns." *Newsweek.* July 28, 1975.

Muggeridge, Malcolm. *Christ and the Media.* Grand Rapids, Mich.: Eerdmans, 1977.

Mumford, Lewis. *Technics and Civilization.* New York: Harcourt, Brace & Jovanovich, 1963.

Myrdal, Gunnar. *Beyond the Welfare State.* New York: Bantam Books, 1967.

Naisbitt, John. *Megatrends.* New York: Warner Books, 1982.

Nash, Roderick. *Wilderness and the American Mind*. Rev. ed. New Haven: Yale University Press, 1973.

Nathanson, Bernard N. *Aborting America*. Garden City, N.Y.: Doubleday, 1979.

Niebuhr, H. Richard. *The Kingdom of God in America*. New York: Harper Torchbooks, 1957.

Nietzsche, Friedrich Wilhelm. "Thus Spake Zarathustra." Vol. I. *Philosophy of Nietzsche*. New York: Modern Library, 1937.

Noll, Mark A. *Christians in the American Revolution*. Washington, D.C.: Christian University Press, 1977.

Noll, Mark A., Nathan O. Hatch, and George M. Marsden. *The Search for Christian America*. Westchester, Ill.: Crossway Books, 1983.

Novak, Michael. *The Experience of Nothingness*. New York: Harper and Row, 1970.

Oliver, Frederick Scott. *Alexander Hamilton: An Essay on American Union*. New York: G. P. Putnam's Sons, 1928.

O'Neill, Catherine. "No Tomorrow: Teen Suicide in America." *Washington Post Health Magazine*. April 23, 1986.

Orwell, George. *Animal Farm* [1946]. New York: New American Library, 1963.

_____. *Nineteen Eighty-Four*. New York: Harcourt, Brace and World, 1949.

Padover, Saul K., ed. *The Complete Jefferson*. New York: Duell, Sloan & Pearce, 1943.

_____. *The Complete Madison*. New York: Harper and Brothers, 1953.

_____. *The World of the Founding Fathers*. New York: Thomas Yoseloff, 1960.

Parrington, Vernon Louis. *Main Currents in American Thought*. New York: Harcourt, Brace, 1927.

Peabody, James Bishop, ed. *John Adams: A Biography in His Own Words*. New York: Newsweek, 1973.

Peikoff, Leonard. *The Ominous Parallels: The End of Freedom in America*. New York: Stein & Day, 1982.

Perry, Ralph Barton. *Puritanism and Democracy*. New York: Vanguard Press, 1944.

Perry, Roland. *Hidden Power: The Programming of the President*. New York: Beaufort Books, 1984.

Perry, William Stevens. *The Faith of the Signers of the Declara-*

tion of Independence. Tarrytown, N.Y.: William Abbatt, 1926.

Peters, Charles. *How Washington Really Works*. Reading, Mass.: Addison-Wesley, 1980.

Peters, Ted. *Futures Human and Divine*. USA: John Knox Press, 1978.

Peterson, Merrill D., ed. *James Madison: A Biography in His Own Words*. 2 vols. New York: Newsweek, 1974.

Phillips, Kevin P. *Post-Conservative America: People, Politics, and Ideology in a Time of Crisis*. New York: Random House, 1982.

Pit, Jan. *Persecution: It Will Never Happen Here?* Orange, Calif.: Open Doors, 1981.

Plato. *Republic*. New York: Basic Books, 1968.

_____. *Laws*. Penguin Books, 1970.

Polanyi, Michael. *Personal Knowledge: Towards a Post-Critical Philosophy*. Chicago: University of Chicago Press, 1958.

_____. *The Tacit Dimension*. New York: Doubleday, 1967.

Postman, Neil. *Amusing Ourselves to Death: Public Discourse in the Age of Show Business*. New York: Viking Press, 1985.

Pound, Roscoe. "Common Law." *Encylopedia of the Social Sciences*. Vol. IV. New York: Macmillan, 1937.

Regulation of the University of Virginia. Chap. 2. Section 1. October 4, 1824.

Reich, Charles. *The Greening of America*. New York: Bantam Books, 1971.

Reichley, A. James. *Religion in American Public Life*. Washington, D.C.: The Brookings Institution, 1985.

Reincourt, Amaury de. *The Coming Caesars*. New York: Coward-McCann, 1957.

Revel, Jean-François. *The Totalitarian Temptation*. Garden City, N.Y.: Doubleday, 1977.

_____. *How Democracies Perish*. Garden City, N.Y.: Doubleday, 1983.

Richardson, James D., ed. *Messages and Papers of the Presidents*. Washington, D.C.: Bureau of National Literature and Art, 1897.

Rifkin, Jeremy. *Algeny*. New York: Viking, 1983.

Robinson, Stuart M. *"And . . . we mutually pledge . . ."* New Canaan, Conn.: The Long House, 1964.

Rookmaaker, H. R. *Modern Art and the Death of a Culture.* Downers Grove, Ill.: InterVarsity Press, 1970.

Rosenfeld, Albert. *The Second Genesis: The Coming Control of Life.* New York: Vintage Books, 1975.

Rosenstock-Huessy, Eugen. *Out of Revolution.* New York: William Morrow, 1938.

Rossiter, Clinton. *Seedtime of the Republic: The Origin of the American Tradition of Political Liberty.* New York: Harcourt, Brace, 1953.

————. *The Political Thought of the American Revolution.* New York: Harcourt, Brace and World, 1963.

Rosten, Leo, ed. *Religions of America.* New York: Simon and Schuster, 1975.

Rousseau, Edward L. "The Intellectual and the American Dream." *Commonweal.* May 1958.

Rousseau, Jean-Jacques. *The Social Contract* [1762]. Reprint. New York: Oxford University Press, 1972.

Runkle, Gerald. *A History of Western Political Thought.* New York: The Ronald Press, 1968.

Rutherford, Samuel. *Lex Rex; or, the Law and the Prince* [1644]. Harrisonburg, Va.: Sprinkle Publications, 1980.

Rutland, Robert Allen. *The Birth of the Bill of Rights, 1776-1791.* Chapel Hill: University of North Carolina Press, 1955.

Sabine, George H. and Thomas L. Thorson. *A History of Political Theory.* 4th ed. Hinsdale, Ill.: Dryden Press, 1973.

Sagan, Eli. *At the Dawn of Tyranny: The Origins of Individualism, Political Oppression, and the State.* New York: Knopf, 1985.

Savage, M. J. *The Religion of Evolution.* Boston: Lockwood, Brooks, 1876.

Scott, Otto J. *Robespierre: The Voice of Virtue.* New York: Mason and Lipscomb, 1974.

————. *The Secret Six: John Brown and the Abolitionist Movement.* New York: Times Books, 1979.

Sealey, Raphael. *A History of the Greek City States, 700-338 B.C.* Berkeley: University of California Press, 1976.

Sennett, Richard. *The Fall of Public Man.* New York: Knopf, 1977.

Shaw, Peter. *The Character of John Adams.* Chapel Hill: University of North Carolina Press, 1976.

Shinn, George. *The American Dream Still Works.* Wheaton, Ill.:

Tyndale House, 1977.

Shirer, William L. *The Rise and Fall of the Third Reich: A History of Nazi Germany.* New York: Simon and Schuster, 1960.

Simon, Julian L. *The Ultimate Resource.* Princeton, N.J.: Princeton University Press, 1981.

Simon, Julian L., and Herman Kahn, eds. *The Resourceful Earth: A Response to Global 2000.* New York: Basil Blackwell, 1984.

Simon, Paul. "American Tune." *Here Comes Rhymin' Simon.* New York: Columbia Records, 1973.

Simon, William E. *A Time for Truth.* New York: McGraw-Hill, 1978.

Singer, C. Gregg. *A Theological Interpretation of American History.* Nutley, N.J.: Craig Press, 1969.

_____. *From Rationalism to Irrationality: The Decline of the Western Mind from the Renaissance to the Present.* Philipsburg, N.J.: Presbyterian and Reformed, 1979.

Sisson, Daniel. *The American Revolution of 1800.* New York: Knopf, 1974.

Skinner, B. F. *Beyond Freedom and Dignity.* New York: Knopf, 1971.

Skinner, Quentin. *The Foundations of Modern Political Thought.* Vol. II. Cambridge: Cambridge University Press, 1978.

Smith, Page. *Jefferson: A Revealing Biography.* New York: American Heritage, 1976.

_____. *The Constitution: A Documentary and Narrative History.* New York: William Morrow, 1978.

_____. *The Nation Comes of Age: A People's History of the Ante-Bellum Years.* Vol. 4. New York: McGraw-Hill, 1981.

Smith, Preserved, ed. *The Life and Letters of Martin Luther.* Boston: Houghton Mifflin, 1911.

Smulders, Peter. *The Design of Teilhard de Chardin.* A. Gibson, trans. Westminster, Md.: Newman Press, 1967.

Solzhenitsyn, Aleksandr I. *August 1914.* New York: Farrar, Straus and Giroux, 1972.

_____. *The Gulag Archipelago, 1918-1956.* New York: Harper and Row, 1973.

_____. *Letter to the Soviet Leaders.* New York: Harper and Row, 1974.

_____. *The Gulag Archipelago, 1918-1956 (Two).* New York:

Harper and Row, 1975.

––––––. "Gulag Survivor Indicts Western 'Freedom.' " *Los Angeles Times*. June 13, 1976.

––––––. *Lenin in Zurich*. New York: Farrar, Straus and Giroux, 1976.

––––––. *The Gulag Archipelago, 1918-1956 (Three)*. New York: Harper and Row, 1978.

––––––. *The Oak and the Calf*. New York: Harper and Row, 1980.

Speer, Albert. *Inside the Third Reich*. New York: Macmillan, 1970.

––––––. *Spandau: The Secret Diaries*. New York: Macmillan, 1976.

––––––. *Infiltration*. New York: Macmillan, 1981.

Spencer, Herbert. *Principles of Sociology* [1880-1897]. 3 vols. Westport, Conn.: Greenwood Press, 1974.

Spengler, Oswald. *The Decline of the West* [1926-1928]. 2 vols. New York: Knopf, 1981.

Spurlin, Paul Merrill. *Montesquieu in America, 1760-1801*. Baton Rouge: Louisiana State University Press, 1940.

Stauffer, Ethelbert. *Christ and the Caesars*. Philadelphia: Westminster Press, 1965.

Stokes, Anson Phelps. *Church and State in the United States*. Vol. I. New York: Harper Brothers, 1950.

Stott, John R. W. *Christ the Controversialist*. Downers Grove, Ill.: InterVarsity Press, 1970.

Stout, Cushing. *The Pragmatic Revolt in American History: Carl Becker and Charles Beard*. Ithaca, N.Y.: Cornell University Press, 1958.

––––––. *The New Heavens and New Earth: Political Religion in America*. New York: Harper and Row, 1974.

Stout, Harry S. *The New England Soul: Preaching and Religious Culture in Colonial New England*. New York: Oxford University Press, 1986.

Symes, Lillian and Clement Travers. *Rebel America*. Boston: Beacon Press, 1972.

Tatarkiewiez, Wladyslaw. *Nineteenth Century Philosophy.* Belmont, Calif.: Wadsworth, 1973.

Tawney, R. H. *Religion and the Rise of Capitalism*. New York: Pelican Books, 1938.

Taylor, Blaine. *The Success Ethic and the Shattered American Dream*. Washington, D.C.: Acropolis Books, 1976.

Teilhard de Chardin, Pierre. *The Phenomenon of Man*. B. Wall, trans. New York: Harper and Row, 1959.

_____. *The Vision of the Past*. J. Cohen, trans. New York: Harper and Row, 1966.

The Presidents Speak: Inaugural Addresses of the Presidents. New York: Holt, Rinehart and Winston, 1969.

Thompson, Dorothy. "The American Dream." *Ladies Home Journal*. July, 1943.

Thoreau, Henry David. *Walden*. Princeton, N.J.: Princeton University Press, 1971.

Thorsmark, Thora. *George Washington*. Chicago: Scott Foresman, 1931.

Tillich, Paul. *Dynamics of Faith*. New York: Harper and Row, 1957.

_____. *Systematic Theology*. 3 vols. Chicago: University of Chicago Press, 1967.

Tipple, John. *Crisis of the American Dream: A History of American Social Thought, 1920-1940*. New York: Pegasus, 1968.

Tocqueville, Alexis de. *Democracy in America* [1835-1840]. Vol. I. New York: Vintage Books, 1954.

Toffler, Alvin. *Future Shock*. New York: Random House, 1970.

_____. *The Eco-Spasm Report*. New York: Bantam Books, 1975.

_____. *The Third Wave*. New York: Bantam Books, 1981.

Turner, Frederick Jackson. *The Significance of the Frontier in American History*. Washington, D.C.: GPO, 1894.

Tuveson, Ernest Lee. *Redeemer Nation: The Idea of America's Millennial Role*. Chicago: University of Chicago Press, 1968.

Twain, Mark. *Autobiography of Mark Twain*. Charles Neider, ed. New York: Harper and Row, 1959.

Unger, Irwin and David Reimers, eds. *The Slavery Experience in the United States*. New York: Holt, Rinehart and Winston, 1970.

VanDoren, Carl. *Benjamin Franklin* [1938]. Reprint. New York: Viking Press, 1980.

Van Tyne, G. H. *Influence of the Clergy on the American Revolution*. American Historical Review. Vol. 14 (1913).

Velikovsky, Immanuel. *Mankind in Amnesia*. Garden City, N.Y.: Doubleday, 1982.

VerSteeg, Clarence L. and Richard Hofstadter, eds. *Great Issues in American History: From Settlement to Revolution, 1584-1776*. New York: Vintage Books, 1969.

Viorst, Milton. *Fire in the Streets: America in the 1960s.* New York: Simon and Schuster, 1979.

Walter, J. A. *The Human Home: The Myth of the Sacred Environment.* Icknield Way, Tring, Herts, England: Lion Publishing Co., 1982.

Walzer, Michael. *The Revolution of the Saints: A Study in the Origin of Radical Politics.* Cambridge: Harvard University Press, 1965.

———. *Exodus and Revolution.* New York: Basic Books, 1985.

Warner, William Lloyd. *American Life.* Chicago: University of Chicago Press, 1962.

Weber, Timothy P. *Living in the Shadow of the Second Coming.* New York: Oxford University Press, 1979.

Weiner, Philip P. *Dictionary of the History of Ideas.* Vol. II. New York: Charles Scribner's Sons, 1973.

Weizenbaum, Joseph. *Computer Power and Human Reason: From Judgment to Calculation.* San Francisco: Walt Freeman, 1976.

Wells, H. G. *The Shape of Things to Come.* New York: Macmillan, 1945.

———. *The Outline of History.* Garden City, N.Y.: Doubleday, 1971.

West, Samuel. *A Sermon Preached Before the Honorable Council and the Honorable House of Representatives of the Colony of Massachusetts Bay.* Boston, 1776.

Whitehead, Alfred North. *The Principles of Natural Knowledge.* Cambridge, England: Cambridge University Press, 1925.

———. *Science and the Modern World.* New York: Macmillan, 1925.

———. *Nature and Life.* New York: Greenwood Press, 1968.

Whitehead, John W. *The Second American Revolution.* Elgin, Ill.: David C. Cook, 1982.

———. *The Stealing of America.* Westchester, Ill.: Crossway Books, 1983.

———. *The Right to Picket and the Freedom of Public Discourse.* Westchester, Ill.: Crossway Books, 1984.

———. *The End of Man.* Westchester, Ill.: Crossway Books, 1986.

Wiedmann, Franz, trans. *Hegel.* New York: Western, 1968.

Wills, Garry. *Inventing America.* Garden City, N.Y.: Doubleday, 1978.

Wilson, Edmund. *Patriotic Gore*. New York: Oxford University Press, 1962.

Wilson, J. O. *Public Schools of Washington*. Vol. 1. Records of the Columbia Historical Society. Washington, D.C.: Columbia Historical Society, 1897.

Wilson, Woodrow. *George Washington* [1896]. Reprint. New York: Schocken Books, 1969.

Wish, Harvey. *Society and Thought in Early America: A Social and Intellectual History of the American People Through 1865*. New York: Longmans Green, 1950.

Woods, David Walker. *John Witherspoon*. Old Tappan, N.J.: Revell, 1906.

Woodward, Kenneth L. "When God Had No Competition: New Insights into the Puritans' Pulpit Culture." *Newsweek*. October 20, 1986.

Woodward, W. E. *A New American History*. New York: Farrar and Rinehart, 1936.

———. *George Washington: The Image and the Man*. New York: Boni and Liveright, 1926.

INDEX